WRITING LETTERS FOR ALL OCCASIONS

HOW TO COMPOSE THE PERFECT LETTER

WRITING LETTERS FOR ALL OCCASIONS

HOW TO COMPOSE THE PERFECT LETTER

JOYCE ROBINS

HAMLYN

Author's Note
The letters contained in this book are a product of
the author's imagination. All the names and addresses
are fictitious and any resemblance to actual events
or persons, living or dead, is entirely coincidental.

First published in 1990 by
The Hamlyn Publishing Group Limited,
a division of the Octopus Publishing Group,
Michelin House, 81 Fulham Road,
London, SW3 6RB

ISBN 0 600 56873 3

Printed and bound in Great Britain by Collins, Glasgow

Contents

Introduction

In these days of telephones and telex, it often seems that the art of letter-writing is dead. Few girls have enough love letters to tie with pink ribbon and friends with news to share are more likely to pick up a telephone than a pen. However, we all need to write letters at some time and then they are important tools. They can persuade an employer to arrange an interview or a creditor to wait for money; they can sell our wares or solve our problems. When writing letters we have time to order our thoughts and strike just the right note, so that a few lines on paper can amuse, intrigue, console, berate or convince.

This book contains more than 250 letters, ranging from a straight-forward booking to an apology after a quarrel or a complaint about school bullies. They cover the formal and informal, the warm and the chilly, both in personal and business correspondence. They are not meant to be copied but, used as a framework for your own thoughts, they can help you to produce the telling word or the persuasive phrase for any occasion.

1

Writing a Letter: the Basics

Any guidelines on the basics of letter-writing – how to begin and end and how to lay out what comes between – tend to sound daunting, or boring, or both. Remember, however, that if your letter is to do its job, it must catch the reader's attention at first glance and give the impression that what you have to say will be worth reading.

A good friend may not mind if your letter has no address or date, if your writing straggles wildly or your signature is an illegible scribble, but anyone else will. A firm that has supplied a defective cooker is far less likely to rush to put things right if your letter looks as though it must have been dashed off by a careless eight-year-old. Your letter does not have to be a literary gem, but to be effective it should look neat and inspire confidence.

Though Auntie Vi may enjoy salmon pink notepaper with a border of forget-me-nots, such a letter is unlikely to galvanize your local councillor into action. Plain, unlined white or cream paper is best for any letter that needs to look businesslike. It is best to type this kind of letter if possible, with your name typed under your signature. Letters are normally typed with single spacing but a very short letter may look better if it is double spaced. It used to be considered bad form to type personal letters, but it is much more acceptable these days and if your writing is difficult to read you will be doing everyone a favour.

Beginning and ending

The correct opening greeting for a letter depends on your degree of intimacy with your correspondent. 'Dear Mr (or Mrs or Miss) Snodgrass' will be the usual formal opening but if you would normally call the recipient by a Christian name, then 'Dear Mildred' or 'Dear Joshua' is appropriate. 'Dear Mildred Snodgrass' or 'Dear Joshua Snodgrass' is sometimes used when writers are not certain about the right note of formality but some people find this objectionable. Surnames alone, as in 'Dear Snodgrass', are not normally used nowadays and though Americans often write 'My Dear Miss Snodgrass', the English find it rather condescending. Only write 'Dear Ms Snodgrass' if you are sure that the woman you are addressing favours this title; otherwise it is more courteous to find out whether Miss or Mrs is correct.

If you want your letter to sound more formal or you have addressed it to 'The Manager' or 'The Marketing Director', then you can use 'Dear Sir' or 'Dear Madam'. When you write to an organization rather than a particular person, then 'Dear Sirs' can be used. 'Sir' or 'Madam' alone is only used in very formal letters, or perhaps when you want to indicate that you are seething with fury. Never begin with 'Dear Sir or Madam', even on a circular. If you do not know the name of the recipient, use 'Dear Sir'. In the case of a circular sent to members of a club or residents' association, 'Dear Member' is a useful substitute and for a round robin to everyone in the office or the works, use 'Dear Colleague'.

When you have used a name in the opening greeting, 'Yours sincerely' is the normal business or formal ending, with 'Yours faithfully' used with a 'Dear Sir' letter. 'Your obedient servant' was once in general use but is now used only when writing formal letters to people of certain ranks. With personal letters you have a far wider choice of ending. You will probably use 'Yours sincerely' when complaining to 'Dear Mr Neighbour' about his objectionably loud radio but writing to a mother who has invited your child to a party might call for a less formal 'Yours' or 'Yours ever'.

Girl friends often use 'With love from' or simply 'Love', as do family members. 'Yours', 'Best wishes' and 'All the best' are more common among men friends and are probably safer between men and women. 'Yours affectionately' is rather old-fashioned now, but may be useful for an elderly aunt.

Laying out letters

The modern style for business letters is blocked. This style has no indentations, no punctuation on the address or on the openings and closings, which are both ranged to the left of the paper. It is supposed to be more arresting and stream-lined and it does look very neat on typewritten letters. Handwritten letters are usually in the gentler looking indented style, with the opening greeting on the left, then each paragraph indented and the closing towards the right hand side of the page. In this style each line of the address, except for the last, is followed by a comma and 'Dear Mr Snodgrass' and 'Yours sincerely' are also followed by commas.

Examples of the two styles are as follows:

SCREW AND BRACKETT
157 Commercial Road Nailham Leeds LG4 7JE

Your ref: ....

12 September 19—

Mr Nicholas Nailer
Manager
Put-It-Up DIY Ltd
Ditchum Trading Estate
Sailbury
Essex
ES5 9TD

Dear Mr Nailer

Order number ....

Thank you very much for your order, which will be dispatched
promptly. I am sure you will find that the goods live up to our usual
high standard.

I enclose a copy of our new catalogue for your information. I would
like to draw your attention to the new range of kitchen shelving, which
I think will be of special interest to you.

If you need any further details, please do not hesitate to contact me.

Yours sincerely

Derek Driller

Derek D. Driller
Sales Director

Enc.

OR

22 July 19—

Dear Justin and Samantha,

I had to write to say how very much I enjoyed the wedding. The bridal party looked really handsome and the colour scheme of dresses and bouquets was beautiful. I took lots of photographs, so I hope you will be able to add some of them to your collection.

There were so many old friends at the reception that I was quite hoarse by the end of the day. I was very glad you chose a buffet, so that we could circulate and catch up on all the news.

Many thanks for asking me to share your special day.

Love,

Hannah

Addressing envelopes

When writing to a man, it is usual to use 'Mr Joshua Snodgrass' in addressing the envelope. The alternative is 'J. Snodgrass Esq.' but this is used far less frequently on modern letters. In business, married women usually prefer their own names or initials, 'Mrs Hyacinth Snodgrass', but in personal correspondence the husband's initials are normally used, 'Mrs J. Snodgrass'. When a woman is divorced, she uses her own Christian name once more. A married woman who uses her maiden name in business is 'Miss Hyacinth Farnzbarn', though some women prefer Ms under these circumstances.

When writing to a firm, you may simply use the firm's name 'Bucket and Sludge Ltd' or precede this with the name of an individual, such as 'The Sales Director'.

The address on the envelope should mirror the style of the letter: either blocked or with each line staggered. For the sake of clarity and quick delivery, the name of the town should be in capitals and the post code in a line of its own, as in the following:

> Mr Nick Nailer
> Manager
> Put-It-Up DIY Ltd
> Ditchum Trading Estate
> Sailbury
> Essex
> ES5 9TD

OR

> Mr and Mrs J. Fitzwarren,
> Chez Nous,
> 53 Orange Blossom Road,
> CHURCHTOWN,
> Dorset,
> DG3 6TF

2

Personal Correspondence

Though a phone call is a quick and easy way to say 'thank you' or 'congratulations', a letter usually means much more to the recipient and the act of sitting down to think about what you want to say means that you can put difficult sentiments into just the right words. Personal letters are normally written by hand and should be sent promptly. Three lines written immediately after an examination success or the arrival of a present is worth far more than a fulsome letter a month later.

The golden rule for personal letters, whether they are thank-yous, congratulations, apologies or condolences, is that they must be sincere. They should never sound as though they are written according to a formula or dashed off along with a dozen others. If you have trouble with 'bread and butter' letters, try to put yourself in the shoes of the recipient. If you have to say 'thank you' for a gift that you know you will never use, see it through the eyes of the sender and remark on the lovely colour, the unusual design or the time and care they must have spent in choosing it. If you are trying to mend a relationship with an apology, whether to a neighbour or a lover, try to imagine what would smooth your ruffled feelings to make you feel better in the same position.

Letters of sympathy and condolence can be the most difficult of all to write but they can also be very important in supporting and comforting someone who is suffering. Never hang back because you feel there is nothing useful to be said; you are telling people that you care about them and that may be the most useful thing you can do in the circumstances.

When you are writing to someone who is ill and you are not sure how serious the illness may be, keep your remarks general. A patient suffering from a terminal illness should not have to read that you hope he will soon be feeling his old self, and someone who expects to recover in a couple of weeks will not appreciate a worried and sombre tone. A friend or relative who is confined to bed may appreciate a newsy letter, but a letter of condolence should always be brief and deal with one subject only. Two or three short paragraphs is as much as the bereaved person will want to read. Simple language is usually best and clichés like 'sad demise', 'your beloved wife' and 'happy release' should be avoided.

Thank you letters

Thanking a friend for a Christmas present

Dear Sid and Shirley,

We were thrilled with the handsome photograph album. It's just what we need for all our really special family pictures and we'll have a lot of fun sorting and selecting them.

I hope your Christmas was as happy as ours – my bathroom scales tell me I enjoyed it all far too much. It would be good to see you soon. I'll give you a ring early in the New Year to make arrangements.

Love,
Don and Doreen

Thanking an acquaintance for a wedding present

Dear Mr and Mrs Murgatroyd,

Ann and I were delighted with such a useful and practical wedding gift. In my bachelor flat the smell of burnt toast was a regular morning feature and now that will be a thing of the past!

Thank you very much for thinking of us on our special day.

Yours,
Nicholas Chan

Thanking a relative for money

Dear Uncle Cyril,

Thank you so much for the cheque; it really was very generous of you. I shall have lots of fun deciding how to spend it. At the moment I'm torn between a personal stereo or a new programme for my computer.

Believe it or not, I'm working quite hard at the moment, with the exams coming in a few weeks' time, so I will write a more newsy letter once they are over and look forward to seeing you in the holidays.

Love,
Darren

Thanking a friend for a christening present

Dear Beryl,

The christening mug is really beautiful; thank you so much for choosing such a lasting present. When Christopher is old enough to appreciate it, I know that it will become a treasure.

I was sorry you couldn't come to the christening but I know it is a brute of a journey. It all went very well and though Christopher objected to being splashed with water and gave a tremendous yell, he let himself be passed from hand to hand among the relatives afterwards without a murmur.

I hope you will get to see him before too long. He's very lively and inquisitive and loves visitors.

Love,
Dawn and Desmond

Thanking a friend for flowers sent to an invalid

Dear Mo and Maurice,

Thank you so much for the beautiful flowers you sent me in hospital. They made such a difference to the ward and I spent a lot of time watching how the light changed the colours.

I would have written sooner but I was flat on my back for a while and writing was impossible. It was good to know that you were thinking about me and I am really grateful for your good wishes.

Love,
Gerry

Thanking friends for a weekend's hospitality

Dear Ben and Beatrice,

Thank you so much for a really happy weekend. It was lovely to escape from the city and relax with you in such a lovely setting. We do appreciate the trouble you took to make us comfortable and feed us splendidly. It was good to see the children again and we specially enjoyed the Sunday ramble through the woods with them.

We shall look forward to your weekend with us in the summer and hope that we can make it as enjoyable as our stay with you.

> Love,
> Ed and Eileen

Thanking friends for helping out in a crisis

Dear Alec and Edna,

I felt I must write and thank you for all that you did for Mavis during her illness. It was a very difficult time but knowing that we could always turn to you made an enormous difference. I particularly remember the day you came and took over completely, so that I could get some much needed sleep.

Of course, I miss her terribly but I would not have wanted her to go on suffering when nothing could be done to help her. It has been a great comfort to have friends who were not embarrassed to talk about her and who had shared so many experiences with us.

> Much love,
> Frank

Apologies

Apologizing to a neighbour

Dear Mr Household,

I must apologize for the behaviour of my son and his friends. I know how much time and trouble you take over the plants in your greenhouse and appreciate how infuriating it was when a carelessly kicked football crashed through the glass.

Believe me, I shall do my best to see that nothing like this ever happens again. In the meantime, please send me the bill for replacing the glass and for any plants that have been damaged.

> Yours sincerely,
> Norman Nipper

OR

Dear Mr Household,

I am so sorry that you were disturbed by our party on Saturday. It was such a warm night that guests spilled out into the garden, doors and windows were flung open and we did not realize that the noise level had risen so high until you phoned.

It was a very special occasion – our silver wedding – so it will be a long time before we hold another party. Please accept this bottle of wine along with my apology.

> Yours sincerely,
> Norman Nipper

Apologizing to a friend for missing a date

Dear Julie,

I'm really sorry I had to call off our date on Saturday. I had a nasty bout of food poisoning – I blame a cheap curry from the night before – and wasn't in a fit state to talk to anyone, let alone go out to dinner. Dad said he would let you know but he can be quite brusque on the phone so I hope he didn't give the wrong impression.

I was very disappointed to miss spending the evening with you and would be very pleased if we could fix another date as soon as possible. As soon as I feel reasonably normal again, I will telephone to make arrangements.

Again, many apologies.

> Love,
> Melvyn

Apologizing to a friend after a quarrel

Dear Sybil,

I am writing to apologize for the unpleasant things I said to you yesterday. I know that I hurt your feelings and that's something I would never do willingly. At the time, there seemed to be nothing I could say to put things right but I would hate to think that my stupid flash of temper might ruin our friendship.

I do hope you will forgive and forget. Let's meet soon – I'll ring in a couple of days and see if we can fix something.

> Love,
> Dorothy

Happy occasions

Announcing an engagement to relatives

Dear Uncle Wilf and Auntie Flo,

I am writing to tell you some fantastic news. I am engaged to be married and planning a spring wedding. My fiancé's name is Darren Duckett and we met a couple of months ago when I went to work at Pringle and Phipps. We have only been going out together for about five weeks so it has all happened very quickly.

I know you will like him once you get a chance to meet and I hope it will be soon.

> Love,
> Hayley

Congratulating a relative on an engagement

Dear Hayley,

Many congratulations on your engagement. It certainly came as a surprise, but a very happy one, and we shall look forward to meeting Darren. If he's the man you have chosen, then how could we help but like him?

We both wish you all the luck and joy in the world. We've always been very proud of you and we know that you will make your husband-to-be very happy.

With love,
Uncle Wilf and Auntie Flo

Congratulating a friend on an engagement

Dear Fay,

I was very excited to hear your news. Congratulations to you both. I thought from the very beginning that this was something special and I'm chuffed to be proved right.

I think you'll make a terrific couple and I wish you lots and lots of happiness. I'll look forward to hearing all your wedding plans.

Love,
Jackie

Asking a friend to be a bridesmaid

Dear Chrissie,

I am writing to ask if you will be chief bridesmaid at my wedding. We have just fixed the date as 22 July and I know your term is over by then. Do say yes – it would mean a lot to me!

I promise you won't have to wear any frills and flounces. My dress will be very simple and the other two bridesmaids are little cousins, aged eight and nine, so you can choose your own style. If you agree we could go on a shopping spree at Easter and choose the material. Mum will make up the dresses and you know what a good dressmaker she is.

I'll be waiting on tenterhooks until I hear that you can accept.

Love,
Fay

Asking a friend to be best man

Dear Sam,

Fay and I have fixed a date for our wedding as 22 July and I'd be really pleased if you would be my best man. Who else could I depend on to see that I get there sober and on time and that no-one fills our going-away cases full of unmentionables? The reception will be small and informal so we won't need any set speeches – a simple toast will be quite sufficient.

I hope you'll be able to say yes.

Yours ever,
Peter

Inserting an engagement announcement in a newspaper

Dear Sir,

Please insert the following announcement in the 'Engagements' section of the Portsend Examiner on Friday 10 June.

The engagement is announced between Justin Michael, only son of Mr and Mrs Sebastian Selkirk of Carlisle and Gemma Alice, younger daughter of Dr and Mrs Patrick Purdy of The Cedars, Manor Crescent, Portsend.

I enclose a cheque for £...

Yours faithfully,
Joan Purdy

Inserting a wedding announcement in a newspaper

Dear Sir,

Please insert the following announcement in the 'Marriages' column of next Saturday's edition.

The marriage between Wade Samuel, elder son of Mr and Mrs Dudley Black of Downtown and Sabrina, only daughter of Mr and Mrs James Smith of Chez Nous, Rosebud Close, Portsend, will take place on Saturday 22 July at St Matthew's Church, Portsend.

I enclose a cheque for £...

Yours faithfully,
Sally Smith

Announcing the birth of a baby to relatives

Dear Uncle Bert,

I know you'll be delighted to hear that our daughter, Zara Elizabeth, arrived at 2 am on Tuesday morning, weighing in at 7lb 12 oz. Of course, we think she's the most beautiful baby in the world.

Pam is very well and happy, after standing up to a long labour rather better than I did. We'll hope to see you soon, to show off the newest member of the family.

> Much love,
> Nick

Congratulating a relative on the birth of a baby

Dear Nick,

Thank you very much for finding the time to write and tell me the news when you must be so busy. Congratulations to you both and all my best wishes for a happy future for Zara Elizabeth. With you and Pam for parents, she can't go wrong.

I shall look forward to seeing her in three weeks' time when I'm spending the weekend with Albert and Gladys. I shall be bringing something suitable to wet the baby's head.

> Love,
> Uncle Robert

Congratulating a friend on the birth of a baby

Dear Nick,

Congratulations! I bet you are a proud Mum and Dad. Of course, you're only beginners, not like us old hands, but there's nothing quite like the first time, so make the most of it. When Alexander arrived we kept feeling his fingers and toes and marvelling that they were real.

We would love to call in at the weekend. Would mid-afternoon on Saturday be O.K. with you?

Look forward to seeing all three of you.

> Lots of love,
> Linda and David

Sending congratulations on a silver wedding

Dear Dick and Jean,

We had to write to wish you happiness on your silver wedding anniversary and send you many congratulations.

Twenty-five years is quite a score and it's hard to believe so much time has passed since that beautiful summer day when you married. We thought then that you would make a splendid couple and the years have proved us right.

Have a wonderful day.

> Love,
> Sylvia and Sam

Sending congratulations on passing an exam

Dear Nigel,

Congratulations on your impressive results. Your Dad said they were even better than he had hoped but it's no more than you deserve after all your hard work.

We are both very proud of you and hope that this is just the beginning of many successes for you.

> Much love,
> Uncle Wilf and Auntie Flo

Sending congratulations on gaining a university place

Dear Scott,

I was so pleased to hear that you got your place at Sussex. All the grind proved worthwhile, didn't it? I'm sure you've chosen the right university and will enjoy every minute of it.

Congratulations and the best of best wishes for a really great three years.

> Yours,
> Alastair

Replying to congratulations on an achievement

Dear Alastair,

Thank you very much for your good wishes. I must say, my main feeling is relief that it's all settled at last. My Dad is so pleased you'd think he had won the pools.

I'm looking forward to it tremendously, especially as Anthony will be going up at the same time so there will be at least one familiar face.

Once I have settled in you must come down for a weekend. It's high time I heard all your news.

Yours,
Scott

Sending congratulations on a child's achievement

Dear Matt and Mabel,

I've just heard that Jason has been selected for the county swimming team and am writing to congratulate you all. You must feel thrilled for him and you should feel really proud of yourselves, too. I know how much time and trouble you have put in to give him the backing he needs.

Do tell Jason how impressed we are. We'll do our best to be there to cheer him on at the first big event.

Love,
Muriel

Replying to congratulations on a child's achievement

Dear Muriel,

It was very kind of you to take such an interest in Jason's swimming prowess. He's so excited, I tell him that his big head will get stuck in the doorway.

Seriously, though, he has worked so hard that he deserves his little bit of glory. We'll certainly let you know when to come and cheer.

Love,
Matt and Mabel

Sad occasions

Sending news of a relative's terminal illness

Dear Maisie,

I find this hard to explain by phone so I decided to write to tell you that John was taken into hospital four days ago. He has terminal cancer and is not expected to live more than a few weeks.

John insisted on knowing the full truth and has been very calm and brave. As there is nothing more the hospital staff can do for him, he will be coming home at the weekend.

I know you haven't seen much of one another over the past few years but I'm sure he would love to see you if you could manage a visit.

Yours,
Dot

Writing to a friend who is seriously ill

Dear Desmond,

We were so sorry to hear about your illness. It's rotten luck, coming just after retirement when you should be able to relax and enjoy life.

Joan says you don't feel much like seeing people at the moment but I hope that changes before too long as we are missing you a lot. We shall be thinking of you and willing an improvement.

Love,
Fred and Dulcie

Writing to a wife whose husband is terminally ill

Dear June,

We have only just heard about Don's illness and it came as a terrible shock. The last time we met he seemed so fit and well.

You must be having a very hard time at the moment and we should like to help if possible. Please tell us if there is anything we can do.

Love,
Al and Annie

Writing to a colleague in hospital

Dear Stan,

I am writing on behalf of everyone on the fourth floor to say how sorry we were to hear that you had been rushed to hospital. I rang Pat this morning and she tells me that you are much more comfortable since the operation and will be sitting up and receiving visitors shortly.

In the meantime, we hope you like the fruit. One or two people did suggest that a case of booze would be far more acceptable but the older and wiser among us insisted that it wouldn't be appropriate.

We'll keep your desk dusted and hope to see you back among us very soon.

>Yours,
>Dave Denning

Responding to a letter of sympathy

Dear Jim and Jean,

I did appreciate your sympathetic letter. I told Gillian that I had heard from you and she sends her love. Some days she is quite alert and interested in what is going on around her, then other days she sleeps all the time.

It's kind of you to offer to help but at the moment we are coping reasonably well and the neighbours have been marvellous. However, if we do need a hand later on, I will certainly let you know.

>Love,
>Arthur

Responding to a letter of sympathy on behalf of a patient

Dear Fred,

Albert asks me to thank you very much for your good wishes. Sitting up long enough to write a letter is more than he can manage at the moment but he is definitely on the mend and we hope that he will be home from hospital in two or three weeks.

So far, only the family have been visiting but by next week, he should be fit enough to enjoy a visit from an old friend and I'm sure there's no-one he would rather see.

Yours,
Win

OR

Dear Fred,

It was very kind of you to write to Albert with your good wishes. I read the letter to him and I can tell he is pleased to know that his friends are thinking of him.

I only wish I could report an improvement but I'm afraid that isn't going to happen. All the same, he is remarkably patient and cheerful.

Yours,
Win

Responding to a letter of sympathy from a colleague

Dear Dave,

I would like to send my thanks to everyone on the fourth floor for the magnificent basket of fruit. It's very kind of you all to think of me. There's enough fruit to feed the whole ward and I've been very popular with the nurses since it arrived.

Booze would probably have been popular too, but it would never have got past sister. She can smell contraband at 100 paces.

I'm feeling more like myself now and it won't be long before I'm back in the commuter crush. Thanks again for all your trouble.

Yours,
Stan

Expressing sympathy after a miscarriage

Dear Janet,

Bob phoned to tell us the sad news. I know how thrilled you were about the baby and what a terrible disappointment it must be.

There's very little anyone can say to help when something like this happens but we do feel for you.

We don't want to intrude if you would rather be on your own but remember that we are here if you want company. Give us a ring or drop in any time.

Love,
Mark and Anna

Sending sympathy to a friend on the death of his wife

Dear James,

I was so sorry to hear of Muriel's sudden death. It must have come as a terrible shock to you and we do feel for you at such a sad time. We shall always remember Muriel as a kind, loving person and the sort of friend you could always count on in a crisis. We shall miss her badly.

If there is anything we can do, or you feel like talking to someone, please give us a call.

Love,
Joan and Arthur

Replying to a friend's letter of condolence

Dear Joan and Arthur,

Thank you very much for your letter and your kind words. There's no way I can tell you how I feel about losing Muriel but it is a great comfort to know how many good friends she had. Letters and cards have been pouring in and I am really touched by the warmth of feeling in them.

Love,
James

Sending sympathy to a relative on the death of her husband

Dear Auntie Vi,

We were very sad to hear about Uncle Larry's death after such a long illness. Though we all knew that it was only a matter of time, it must be a very difficult period for you.

We shall see you at the funeral on Friday and wonder if you would like to come home with us for a few days afterwards. Don't feel pressured into coming if you would rather be at home but if you would like some company, you will be very welcome.

Love,
Max and Margaret

Replying to a relative's letter of condolence

Dear Max and Margaret,

Very many thanks for your kind letter. I don't think I've really taken it all in yet. It's so hard to believe that Larry has gone but he was in a very bad way in the last few weeks so at least he won't have to suffer any more.

It's very thoughtful of you to ask me to stay but at the moment I need to stay at home and try to get used to what has happened. I have plenty of friends round here and they have all been very kind.

Love,
Auntie Vi

Notifying a friend about a death

Dear Jill,

I have very sad news to tell you. Jack died yesterday at St Mary's Hospital after a short illness. It came as a terrible shock, as the doctors hoped he would pull through, right up to the last couple of days. He stayed cheerful and, thankfully, seemed unaware of how ill he was.

The funeral is on Tuesday at 11 am at St Saviour's, the church in the High Street. I'm sure Jack would have liked you to come, if you can.

Love,
Marian

Letter of reply to news about a death

Dear Marian,

I was really upset to get your letter with your sad news. It's almost impossible to believe that we have lost Jack. He was always so full of life and fun. Wherever he was, there were always happy faces.

Certainly I shall be at the funeral but I wonder if there's something more that I can do. I am free all next week so if there's any way at all I can help, don't hesitate to let me know.

Love,
Jill

Formal expression of condolence to the widow of a colleague

Dear Mrs Soper, (*or* Dear Anne, *if appropriate*),

We were so sorry to hear the sad news of Tony's death. He was a valued colleague and will be sorely missed. I have received several letters of tribute from our customers and I will send these on to you.

The directors join me in expressing their condolences.

Yours sincerely,
Selwyn Smith

Formal expression of condolence from an acquaintance

Dear Anne,

I was very sorry to read in the paper of Tony's death and I am writing on behalf of all the members of the snooker team to express our deep sympathy.

I assure you that our thoughts are with you in this trying time.

Yours sincerely,
Percy Jones

Formal reply to a letter of condolence

Dear Mr Smith,

Thank you very much for your kind letter and expression of sympathy. It helps to know how many friends Tony had made through his work. He will be missed by so many people.

Yours sincerely,
Anne Soper

Inserting a death announcement in a newspaper

Dear Sir,

Please include the following announcement in the 'Deaths' column of your newspaper in the earliest possible edition.

SEDGWICK– On 7 January peacefully at the Eventide Nursing Home, Townsend, Lilian Adelaide, widow of Percival. Funeral service at St Cuthbert's Parish Church, 2 pm Friday 10 January. Flowers to A. Green, 11 Brook Road, Downtown.

I enclose a cheque for £....

Yours faithfully,
Anthony Green

Alternative wording for death announcement

TATNELL – On 22 September at home in Storyville, near Portsend, Cecil George, beloved husband of Edith and father of Roger and Isabel. Cremation has taken place.

OR

LEVER – On 6 May after a long illness Frederick John. Sadly missed by his wife and family. Funeral service at Downtown Crematorium on 10 May at 11.30 am. Family flowers only. Donations to St Cecilia's Hospice.

3

Practical Matters

Letters on practical matters, whether they are making an offer to buy a property or excusing a child from PE lessons, need to be short and direct. They should go straight to the heart of the subject so that the reader can absorb them quickly and easily, thus maximizing your chances of achieving the result you want. Too much verbiage can mean that the most important request or piece of information in your letter is missed altogether if it is read hurriedly.

Confine yourself to a single subject whenever possible. If, for instance, you are asking the landlord to wait a little longer for the rent, don't get side-tracked into mentioning the dripping guttering or the rudeness of his secretary when you try to reach him by phone. Settle the most important issue first, then, if you have other matters to discuss, write a second letter.

Writing to a child's head teacher, or to the local council, often causes problems to those who seldom put pen to paper, but remember that no-one will be impressed by long words and stilted phases and the simpler you keep your letter, the better. Try not to be so curt that the letter sounds rude and aggressive, but there is no need to sound apologetic or grovelling either. If you write as though you were addressing an equal, you will usually receive a reply in the same vein.

Buying and selling a house

Requesting particulars from an estate agent

Dear Sirs

I am planning to move to Portsend and would be grateful if you could send particulars of semi-detached or terraced houses in the £60,000-80,000 price bracket.

The accommodation must include three bedrooms of reasonable size and must be within walking distance of the town centre.

Yours faithfully
Roger M. Blenkinsop

Confirming an arrangement with an estate agent to handle a sale

Dear Mr Squibb

Following our conversation this morning, I confirm that Squibb and Sprunt will handle the sale of 73 Costly Crescent as sole agents and that your commission will be 2 per cent of the selling price, plus VAT. No further charge will be made for any adverts placed by your firm.

I also confirm that the sole agency will last for three months, after which the situation will be reviewed. However, if the house is sold as a result of my own efforts, to a buyer not introduced through your firm, no fee will be payable.

Yours sincerely
Louise Percy (Mrs)

OR

Dear Mr Squibb

I write to confirm that Squibb and Sprunt will handle the sale of 73 Costly Crescent on a multiple agency basis at a commission of 3 per cent of the selling price, plus VAT.

As I mentioned, I do not wish to have a 'For Sale' board outside the house though I have no objection to a 'Sold' notice, erected by the firm which succeeds in selling the property.

Yours sincerely
Louise Percy (Mrs)

Confirming an arrangement with a solicitor's property centre

Dear Mr Small

I wish to confirm that Downtown Solicitors' Property Centre will handle the sale of my house at 96 Woodlands Avenue, also the conveyancing on this property and on 24 Lancaster Road, on which my offer has been accepted and a deposit lodged.

I note that your estimated bill will be £... This amount is to include legal fees and commission, with expenses and VAT payable in addition.

Yours sincerely
Fanny Flower (Miss)

Inserting a house advertisement in a newspaper

Dear Sir

Please include the following advertisement in the property column of your Classified Advertisements for two days on Thursday and Friday, 2-3 May.

DOWNTOWN Detached Regency style house, 3 double bedrooms, large through sitting/dining room, newly re-fitted kitchen. Gas central heating, large garage, well-stocked garden. £120,000 FH. Tel .....: evenings.

I enclose a cheque for £...

Yours faithfully
Christopher Crisp

Confirming an offer to purchase to an estate agent

Dear Mr Squibb

73 Costly Crescent

I wish to confirm my verbal offer of £75,000 on the above property, SUBJECT TO CONTRACT AND SURVEY.

As I told the vendor, Mrs Percy, I am negotiating with a buyer on my own house and am hoping for an early completion date.

Yours sincerely
Gerald Gonk

Making an offer to purchase in a private sale

Dear Mr Goodbody

Thank you for showing me over your house yesterday. I should like to make an offer of £67,000, subject to contract and survey. This price would include fitted carpets and curtains.

I realize that this is below your asking price but, as I mentioned when we met, I am a first time buyer with a mortgage already agreed 'in principle' by the building society, so there is no chain involved and no reason for any delays or hitches.

Please let me know if you are prepared to accept.

Yours sincerely
Geoffrey Hopeful

Accepting an offer to purchase in a private sale

Dear Mr Hopeful

Thank you for your letter of 22 May. I am willing to accept your offer of £67,000 for 52 Squirrel Close but, as this is £2,500 below the asking price, I could not include carpets and curtains.

If you wish to make a separate offer for carpets and curtains, I shall be glad to consider it.

Yours sincerely
Gerald Goodbody

Rejecting an offer to purchase in a private sale

Dear Mr Hopeful

Thank you for your interest in my property but I have to reject your offer of £67,000.

At the moment I have several interested prospective buyers and anticipate no difficulty in obtaining the asking price.

Yours sincerely
Gerald Goodbody

Confirming arrangements with conveyancer on house purchase

Dear Miss Dainty

Purchase of 52 Squirrel Close

This is to confirm that you will handle the conveyancing of the above property for a fixed fee of £... plus VAT.

The vendor's name is Gerald Goodbody and I understand that he is handling his own conveyancing. I enclose a copy of my offer to purchase and the vendor's acceptance, also a list of fixtures and fittings agreed with Mr Goodbody when I visited the property. We have also agreed on a price of £350 for carpets and curtains.

Yours sincerely
Geoffrey Hopeful

Confirming arrangements with solicitor on sale and purchase

Dear Mr Surely

<u>Sale of 6 Myrtle Road, Downtown</u>

<u>Purchase of 29 Church Road, Portsend</u>

I write to confirm that you will be handling the conveyancing on the above sale and purchase and that your estimated fee for the two transactions is £...

The buyers of 6 Myrtle Road are Mr and Mrs R. Patel of 45 Loftus Road, Streetford. Their solicitors are Clapper and Clinch, 25 Commercial Road, Streetford.

The vendor of 29 Church Road is Mr T. R. Bagshaw. His solicitors are Fogwell, Fogwell and Cramp, 117 Brackwell Road, Portsend.

I would be obliged if the transactions could be handled as speedily as possible.

Yours sincerely
Christopher Crisp

Planning permission

Enquiring about planning permission

Dear Sir

I am hoping to convert the loft at the above address into an extra bedroom.

As far as I know, this type of work does not require planning permission. Would you please confirm this?

Yours faithfully
Horace Household

Re-submitting an application for planning permission after permission has been refused

Dear Sir

In February I applied for planning permission for an extension to the above address. At the time permission was refused because the proposed extension would have altered the general line of the buildings in the road. I have now had the plans re-drawn so that this is no longer the case and wish to make a fresh application.

I understand that, as my revised application is made within 12 months of the first application, I do not have to pay another fee. I trust that I shall be successful this time.

Yours faithfully
Horace Household

Objecting to the planning department about a neighbour's planning application

Dear Sir

Application No. 567 for extension at 6 The Avenue

I wish to lodge an objection to the extension proposed at the above address.

I have inspected the plans in the planning register and find that the angle of the extension means that it will look directly into my living room, at a distance of only a few feet. I would only be able to retain any privacy by keeping curtains drawn and living in semi-darkness.

This would interfere with my enjoyment of my own property and reduce its value, so I trust that the application will be rejected.

Yours faithfully
Alan Anger

Writing to the planning enforcement officer about a neighbour's building work, begun without permission

Dear Sir

32 Offshoot Road

I feel I must notify you that my neighbour at the above address, Mr

Tacky, is converting his house into several flats, with the intention of living in one and letting the rest.

On checking with the planning department, I find that no planning permission has been granted or sought. Therefore I would ask you to take immediate action to ensure that this work does not take place.

Any planning application for a change of use of this nature would meet with strong opposition from a number of residents in Offshoot Road.

Yours faithfully
Roland Righteous

Bookings and estimates

Booking a hotel

Dear Sir

I should like to book a double room for my wife and myself for seven nights from 9 September to 15 September inclusive. We would require a room with twin beds and sea view. Please let me know the price per person for dinner, bed and breakfast for this period.

Perhaps you could also let me know the names of any water sports firms in the area who could give tuition in wind surfing and water-skiing.

Yours faithfully
Toby Trott

Confirming a hotel booking

Dear Mr Bedwell

I am writing to confirm my booking of a twin-bedded room with sea view for seven nights from 9 September to 15 September.

Thank you for sending so much useful information on water sports firms.

Yours sincerely
Toby Trott

Confirming a telephone booking

Dear Mrs Welcome

I am writing to confirm my telephone booking of a four-berth caravan at Cosy Corner Caravan Park for one week, beginning on 6 August. As we discussed, we shall require a caravan in a quiet situation, well away from the road.

I enclose a cheque for £25 as a deposit.

Yours sincerely
Carol Camper

Following up an advertisement for holiday cottages

Dear Sir

Further to your advertisement in the Downtown Gazette, please forward particulars and prices of holiday cottages available on the North York Moors during August.

My family will need sleeping accommodation for five. We shall also be bringing two spaniels so we can only consider accommodation where pets are accepted.

Yours faithfully
Jill Judd (Mrs)

Booking a tailor-made holiday through a travel agent

Dear Mr Fixer

Following our telephone conversation I confirm that I wish you to make the following bookings for a holiday in Israel for two adults and two children.

1. Flights on scheduled airlines from Heathrow to Tel Aviv and return: outward journey Saturday 14 October, homeward journey Saturday 28 October.

2. Accommodation in first class hotels in two double rooms on a bed and breakfast basis as follows:
    October 14 Tel Aviv (1 night)
    October 15-18 Jerusalem (4 nights)
    October 19-26 Dead Sea (8 nights)
    October 27 Tel Aviv (1 night)

3. A hire car (regular family saloon size) to be collected at the airport on 14 October and returned there at the end of the holiday.

Yours faithfully
Edward Eccleston

Arranging for hire of removal van

Dear Sir

I wish to hire a rental van of a suitable size to carry the contents of a small terraced house. Please supply details of your hire charges and mileage rates and what insurance cover is included or available.

I should prefer a van with a tail lift but if this is not possible, then a ramp is essential.

Yours faithfully
Christopher Crisp

Accepting a quote for removal and confirming terms

Dear Mr Mover

Your quote of £... for the packing and removal of my household effects from 17 Spring Gardens to 93 Tenby Terrace is acceptable and I look forward to seeing your removal team by 8 am on Tuesday 10 May.

Further to our telephone conversation, I confirm that you will provide covers for the furniture in case of rain and hanging wardrobes for clothes.

Yours sincerely
Jacqueline Jolly

Requesting an estimate for home improvements

Dear Sir

I would be grateful if you could give me an estimate for re-fitting a bathroom, including wall tiling, new bathroom suite and installation of an electric shower. I attach a list of fixtures and fittings to be included in the work.

Would it be possible for your representative to call on a weekday evening or a Saturday to assess the job in detail? Perhaps you could also give me a possible starting date. I would need the work completed some time within the next two months.

Yours faithfully
Horace Household

Confirming acceptance of an estimate for home improvements

Dear Mr Bricker

Thank you for sending your estimate for work on my house extension.

The amount of £... is acceptable, so I confirm that you will be starting work on 5 June and that the job will be completed by 1 July.

It is also part of our contract that the cost of the work as given in your estimate will not be exceeded without my permission.

Yours sincerely
Edward Eccleston

School and education authorities

Asking a head teacher for an appointment

Dear Mr Screech,

I am very concerned over Jason's poor progress in reading. At seven years old he still stumbles over the simplest words and is unable to read books directed at children in his age group.

I would like to make an appointment to talk to you and to Jason's class teacher, Miss Young, about the problem. I would appreciate your views on whether some form of extra tuition is needed at this stage.

Yours sincerely,
Angela Anger

Writing to a head teacher about problems at home

Dear Mrs Pentecost,

I feel that I should tell you that Stacey is going through a very upsetting time at the moment and I hope that, if her school work is suffering, you will understand and make allowances.

My husband left home three months ago and divorce proceedings have begun. Though I have tried to keep life as normal as possible for Stacey, her father is very bitter and there are times when she must feel as though she is in the middle of a tug of war.

She prefers not to talk about it and I would be surprised if she has mentioned any of this at school but she does get very upset and finds it difficult to concentrate. Yesterday evening I found her in floods of tears over her maths homework because, in her emotional state, she could make no headway with it.

I hesitated to write, as I know Stacey would be unhappy to think that her problems were widely known. However, I feel that trouble at school over poor work would be the last straw for her. I know that I can rely on your understanding and discretion.

> Yours sincerely,
> Hannah Hubble

Writing to a head teacher about bullying

Dear Mr Jolly,

Three times this week my son Patrick, who is in form 2A, has come home very hungry because his lunch money was extorted from him by older boys, with threats of beatings.

There seem to be several fourth years who regularly lie in wait for the younger boys at the side of the building, near the science laboratories, and force them to hand over their cash. I have talked to two of Patrick's friends and they tell the same story

I am sure that you are as concerned as I am to have this behaviour stopped and that you will take the necessary measures to see that younger boys are no longer terrorized by these bullies.

> Yours sincerely,
> Pauline Pepper

Writing to a head teacher withdrawing a child from religious education

Dear Mr Wise,

My son David will be joining your first year pupils when term starts next week. As he is a member of the Jewish faith, it is my wish that he withdraws from any class in religious education or any act of collective worship.

Yours sincerely,
Israel Cohen

Writing to a head teacher about pornographic literature circulating in the school

Dear Mr Wise,

I wish to draw your attention to the fact that pornographic literature is circulating freely in the school. I found in Mark's school bag two magazines featuring naked men and women engaged in various sex acts. He tells me that they have been read by most of the boys in his class and were passed down from the third year.

I am sure you will agree that this is an undesirable way for 13-year-old boys to pursue their sex education and I trust that you will be able to stop the circulation of these magazines.

Yours sincerely,
Angus Anxious

Requesting the transfer of a child to another school

Dear Miss Bigg,

My son Frederick has been attending Easytime School for 18 months but he is unhappy there and I am dissatisfied with his progress.

Several of my friends have children at Haughty High School and they all speak very highly of the education they are receiving. As I feel that Frederick will benefit from a more academically based system, I would like him to transfer to your school.

Perhaps you could let me know if there is a place available for him.

Yours sincerely,
Eleanor Eager

Informing a head teacher about plans for a transfer

Dear Mr Dabble,

I have been in touch with Miss Bigg at Haughty High School, enquiring about the possibility of arranging a transfer for Frederick and she has asked me to let you know of my intentions.

As you know from our conversations over the past year, I have been worried over Frederick's lack of progress. I feel that he would benefit from a more strictly structured system and hope that a transfer to Haughty High School can be arranged for the beginning of next term.

Yours sincerely,
Eleanor Eager

Landlord and tenant

Writing to a tenant about overdue rent (polite)

Dear Mrs Felix

I write to remind you that the half yearly rent on 12 Rundle Road, payable on 1 March, is now overdue. No doubt this is due to an oversight on your part and I shall be pleased to receive your cheque as soon as possible.

Yours sincerely
Gary Grout

Writing to a tenant about overdue rent (pressing)

Dear Mr Brash

The half yearly rent on Flat 4, The Towers, payable on 1 March is now four weeks overdue. As you have been late in paying on the last three occasions, I must insist on immediate payment, otherwise I shall be forced to take further action.

Yours sincerely
Gary Grout

Requesting the landlord to make repairs

Dear Mr Grout

I must draw your attention to the poor state of the upstairs window sills at the above address. These are rotting badly and the damp is penetrating our bedrooms. This is very unhealthy for our three-year-old son and eight-month-old daughter.

Please arrange for the necessary repairs as a matter of urgency.

Yours sincerely
Norman Nipper

Applying to the Rent Officer to fix a fair rent

Dear Sir

I have been renting a two-roomed flat at 12 Swindles Road for two months and paying £60 a week in rent. However, I find that the 'going rate' for similar flats in the area is nearer £50, so I wish to apply to register a fair rent. Would you be kind enough to send me the necessary form?

Yours faithfully
Fiona Fagg

Querying maintenance charges with a landlord

Dear Mr Grout

The current bill for maintenance charges on Grotty Court shows a rise of 40 per cent on the previous year. This seems excessive to me and out of all proportion to the amount of work actually done on the building.

Please provide a full breakdown of these charges and an explanation of the increase.

Yours sincerely
Marlene Mapp

Writing to a landlord objecting to proposed charges for decorating

Dear Mr Grout

Thank you for your letter dated 20 March. I am shocked at the amount estimated as my share of the cost of redecorating the building. I note that you have only provided one estimate and I consider that this is far too high.

I would remind you that the law requires that you obtain at least two estimates for any major work and that you give details to the leaseholders at least one month in advance of the undertaking of the work, so that they have time to raise any queries or objections.

Yours sincerely
Sybil Salmon

Requesting a landlord to allow extra time to pay rent

Dear Mr Grout

The rent on the above premises was due on 10 April but I am writing to ask you to allow me two or three extra weeks to find the money.

As you know, I have always paid promptly in the past but I have been ill with a virus infection for the past three weeks and, as I work in a freelance capacity, I have had no income during that time.

I have now been pronounced fit and ready to start work again next week so if I could delay paying the rent for a short time, it would give me the breathing space I need.

Yours sincerely
Cecily Clinch

Serving notice to quit on a tenant

Dear Mr Brash

I the undersigned as landlord hereby give you notice to quit and surrender to me the premises known as Flat 6, Grotty Court on 31 May 1990, being four weeks from the serving of this notice and the date of expiry of your monthly tenancy.

I am required by law to give you the following information:

If the tenant does not leave the dwelling, the landlord must get an order for possession from the court before the tenant can lawfully be evicted. The landlord cannot apply for such an order before the notice to quit has run out.

A tenant who does not know if he has any right to remain in possession after a notice to quit runs out or is otherwise unsure of his rights can obtain advice from a solicitor. Help with all or part of the cost of legal advice and assistance may be available under the Legal Aid Scheme. He should also be able to obtain information from a Citizens' Advice Bureau, a Housing Aid Centre, a Rent Officer or a Rent Tribunal Office.

Yours sincerely
Gary Grout

Applying to the council for the right to buy a council house

Dear Sirs

As a local authority tenant of more than two years standing, I wish to buy my council house. Please send the Right to Buy Claim Form.

Yours faithfully
Henry Hubble

Notifying local authority landlord of an appeal to the District Valuer

Dear Sirs

I must inform you that I consider the price you have set for the purchase of my council house is too high, taking into consideration the area, and so I wish to refer the matter to the District Valuer.

Therefore I wish for a <u>determination of value under section 128 of the Housing Act 1985</u>.

Yours faithfully
Henry Hubble

Requesting the council to allow an exchange of council houses

Dear Sirs

I wish to exchange my council house for a house of identical size in West Sussex and I therefore request your written permission to transfer my tenancy to Mr Samuel Snodgrass of 23 Whiteside Road, Carberry. I am forced to seek a move for reasons of employment.

Mr Snodgrass is, of course, seeking permission for transfer from Windrush District Council. His family, like mine, consists of a wife and two children, so our accommodation requirements are identical.

Yours faithfully
John Brown

Clubs and societies

Suggesting the formation of a residents' association

Dear Mr Batty

Several residents of Grotty Court have suggested that we should form a residents' association. This would assist us in our negotiations with the landlord over essential repairs and might also enable us to work together to improve the communal areas of the building.

I have taken on the task of writing to all residents inviting them to a meeting in Mr McGinty's flat, No. 4, on Tuesday 15 February at 8 pm to discuss the pros and cons of such an association. Please let Mr McGinty or myself know if you can attend. If you are not free to come, we would be interested to know your views on the matter in advance of the meeting.

We shall prepare a full report on the meeting and circularize all residents.

Yours sincerely
Basil Busy

Proposing a new club member

Dear Mr Bunker

I wish to propose Mr Michael Brown for membership of Nobs Golf Club. Mrs Barbara Birdie seconds the nomination. We both know Mr Brown as a keen golfer who has recently moved into the area and will be a real asset to the club.

Yours sincerely
Peter Parr

Applying for club membership

Dear Mr Heart

My husband and I are keen to become members of the Downtown Bridge Club. We have recently returned from a year in Saudi Arabia and we have, as yet, had no opportunity to get to know any of your members, so we have no formal proposers.

However, before leaving England we were living in West Sussex where we belonged to the Carberry Bridge Club and played several times in regional tournaments. I would be pleased to supply the name and address of the secretary.

Perhaps you would be kind enough to bring our names before your committee for consideration.

Yours sincerely
Lyn Spade

Approaching a speaker to address a club meeting

Dear Professor Brain

As secretary of the Downtown Historical Society, I am arranging our programme of speakers for the spring season and wondered if you would be willing to give us a lecture (approximately one hour) on your specialist period, the social history of the Victorian era. We would leave the exact choice of subject up to you.

Many of our members have a particular interest in this period and I am sure we would have a good attendance. We normally have between 50 and 80 people at our meetings.

We meet on Thursday evenings at 8 pm and hope that you might be able to address one of our April meetings. We would of course meet your expenses and hope that you would accept an invitation to dinner before the meeting.

Yours sincerely
Emily East
Secretary

OR

Dear Mr Fame

I am writing to ask if you would consider being our guest speaker at the annual dinner of Nobs Golf Club on Saturday, 13 November. Having had the pleasure of hearing you speak at the Portsend Rotarians dinner last year, I know what a treat would be in store for us.

If you are free on this date, please let me know what fee you would require. We would, of course, pay all expenses in addition.

Yours sincerely
Bernard Bunker
Secretary

Arranging for the arrival of a speaker

Dear Professor Brain

Thank you so much for agreeing to deliver a lecture on 'Middle Class Values in Victorian England' to our society on Thursday 10 April. Our members are looking forward to the evening with keen anticipation.

We usually allow half an hour for questions after the meeting and I hope this will be agreeable to you.

The 5.30 pm train from Paddington arrives in Downtown at 6.15 pm and I will meet you at the station. You should be in good time for the return train at 10 pm.

I have made arrangements for the slide projector to be in place. Please let me know if you will need any other visual aids on the night.

Yours sincerely
Emily East
Secretary

Writing to members asking for donations

Dear Member

I make no apology for writing to all the members of the Old Malhallians Association asking for a donation towards the repair of the school bell tower. Repair and renovation is essential for the safety of the tower, as well as its appearance, and the estimated cost is £...

As this is more than the school funds can reasonably bear, we are launching an appeal, aiming to raise £... by the end of the year.

You will be receiving details of extra events, including a dance and a choral concert, in due course but at the moment we are asking for cheques, postal orders or bank notes. We are sure that you will want to contribute.

Yours faithfully
Stephen Scholar
Secretary

Motoring

Writing to the council, opposing parking meters

Dear Sirs

I understand that the council is considering installing parking meters in Ash Lane and Oak Road, instead of the '30 minutes only' regulation currently in force. I am strongly opposed to this idea and hope that you will reject it.

At the moment, most of the motorists using these roads for parking are shopping in the High Street and stopping for anything from 5 to 30 minutes while they make a few purchases. This means that there is almost always a short-term parking space available.

Meters will encourage far more one and two hour parking, so that shoppers will find it increasingly difficult to park and High Street traders will suffer. The disadvantages for local residents and businesses far outweigh the advantages of the small amount of extra revenue that would be provided by meters.

Yours faithfully
Elsie Anxious

Writing to the Chief Constable following a motoring offence

Dear Sir

On 28 September I was stopped for speeding on Downtown Road and I understand that I may be prosecuted for this offence.

I acknowledge that I had overlooked the speed restriction beginning as the Freeborough Highway becomes Downtown Road and that I was travelling at 50 mph in a 40 mph zone.

At the time, I was on my way to visit my wife in hospital and I fear that I allowed my anxiety about her condition to affect my judgment. At the time the road was clear, visibility was perfect and there was no likelihood of my extra speed causing a hazard to other road users.

I am normally a careful driver and I have an unblemished record over 25 years. In the circumstances I can only hope that you will decide not to go ahead with a prosecution.

Yours faithfully
Lawrence Driver

Pleading guilty to a motoring offence with a letter in mitigation to the court

Dear Sirs

Police v. A. J. Wheel, 10 December 1990

I acknowledge receipt of the summons and plead guilty to failing to comply with traffic signals.

I admit that on 20 November I failed to stop at a red light at the junction of The Street and Downtown Road. The lights were green as I approached the junction and by the time they turned amber I was very near and I had a car driving close behind me. I felt that braking might well cause an accident, so I decided that the safest course was to proceed. I did not realize that the light would turn to red before I crossed the stop line.

I understand that penalty points will be endorsed on my licence, which I enclose. However, I would ask for the leniency of the court in the matter of a fine.

Yours faithfully
A. J. Wheel

OR

Dear Sirs

Police v. P. Streeter, December 10 1990

I acknowledge receipt of the summons and plead guilty to driving my vehicle without a current M.O.T. certificate.

It was not until I was asked by a police officer to produce the certificate, along with my other documents, that I realized it was four weeks out of date. I had overlooked its renewal in the worry and stress of being made redundant when Connie's Casuals went into receivership last September.

After my conversation with the officer I drove directly to the testing centre and obtained the new certificate. I regret the oversight and hope that the court will be lenient. As my only income is unemployment benefit and I have no prospect of another job at present, I would be grateful if I could discharge any fine at £5 a week.

Yours faithfully
Coral Crisp

4

Complaints

If a letter of complaint is to be effective, it must be clear, calm and firm. Even if you are furious about the treatment you have received, your letter needs to be crisp and concise. Though the saga of your building works could fill a book, the recipient of your letter is unlikely to wade through five pages of detail to discover what redress you are seeking. However justified your complaint may be, you will undermine your case if your letter is abusive, hysterical or one long, confused grumble.

Set out your grievances clearly, giving any relevant dates, prices and names. State plainly what you are asking for: an apology, a refund, a replacement, compensation for loss or inconvenience, or action to ensure better standards in future. It is worth a telephone call to the firm or organization involved to find out which department is likely to be able to deal with your complaint, or the name of the manager or managing director. A letter addressed by name is more likely to reach the person you are targeting, rather than being shuffled into an assistant's in-tray.

The more business-like your letter looks, the better. Type it if possible but if it is handwritten, make sure that every word is legible and that the paragraphs are well-spaced. Be prepared to persist if you do not achieve results immediately. In a second letter it may help to set a deadline – say seven days from the date of the letter – after which you will take your complaint higher, refer it to a trade association or begin legal action.

Complaints about goods

Complaint about goods bought from a supermarket

Dear Sir

On Friday 28 August I purchased a 3 lb packet of frozen chicken quarters from your store. When I had defrosted them ready for use on

Sunday 30 August, I found that they had an unpleasant smell and that there were small green patches on the underside of several pieces.

As I was unable to return them to the store within the next 24 hours, and the smell was permeating my refrigerator, I disposed of them. However, I enclose the packet as proof of purchase and would be grateful for a refund of the purchase price of £3.80.

Yours faithfully
M. L. Shopper (Mrs)

Protecting statutory rights over defective goods

Dear Mr Hardcastle

I should like to put on the written record that this morning I returned the Grassguzzler lawnmower bought from you three weeks ago. This ceased to function the third time I used it.

As you assured me that a minor repair would rectify the fault, I have left the machine with you for collection on the morning of 12 May. However, if the repair is not completed to my complete satisfaction, I reserve my statutory rights to a refund of the full purchase price.

Yours sincerely
M. L. Shopper (Mrs)

Claiming for faulty goods

Dear Mr Flack

On 13 October I bought a Super-Duper Iron, Model No... from your shop. Two days later I used it for the first time to press my daughter's dress. Though I used the lowest setting, it left a large scorch mark.

When I returned the iron on 17 October I spoke to your Mr Philpott. He tested it, decided that the temperature control was faulty and offered me a replacement. I felt that, in the circumstances, I must claim recompense for the ruined dress, which had only been worn once. Mr Philpott told me that I should approach you about this on your return from holiday.

The dress cost £30 when I bought it eight weeks ago and I consider that £20 would be a reasonable amount of compensation.

Yours sincerely
M. L. Shopper (Mrs)

Complaint about late delivery of goods ordered from store

Dear Sir

When I ordered matching curtains and bedspread from your store on
3 March, I was told that they would take three weeks to make.

Three weeks later my order had not arrived and I was told that it would
be ready in a week's time. It is now seven weeks since I placed my
order and there is still no sign of my curtains or bedspread.

Unless my goods arrive within 14 days of the date of this letter, I wish
to cancel the order and reclaim my deposit.

Yours faithfully
M. L. Shopper (Mrs)

Complaint about unsolicited goods

Dear Sir

This morning I received a book entitled 'Healthy Eating for Greedy
Guts' through the post, as an introductory offer to the Health Nuts
Book Club, together with an invoice for £4.25.

I did not order this book and I do not wish to join the book club. Please
make arrangements to collect your goods from the above address.

Yours faithfully
Daphne Spender

Complaint to Trading Standards Officer about unsolicited goods

Dear Sirs

On 12 February I received unsolicited goods – a book entitled
'Healthy Eating for Greedy Guts' – from the Health Nuts Publishing
Company, together with an invoice for £4.25.

I wrote two days later asking the company to arrange collection of
these unwanted goods, sending my letter by recorded delivery. Since
then I have received three more demands for payment, which I have
ignored. I enclose a copy of the latest invoice. I should be grateful if
you could take action against this firm, which is obviously engaging in
dubious trading practices.

Yours faithfully
Daphne Spender

Rejecting unsatisfactory mail order goods

Dear Sir

On 13 November I took delivery of a Grill-it-Good Barbecue, ordered through your newspaper advertisement and priced at £25.95.

On assembling the barbecue, I found that it was impossible to screw in the legs securely. In addition, the whole barbecue is extremely flimsy and I could buy a similar item more cheaply in local shops. I therefore reject the barbecue as unsatisfactory and wish to claim a full refund, as promised in your advert. Please tell me if you wish me to return it to you (in which case I shall expect a refund of carriage charges) or if you will collect it.

Yours faithfully
Daphne Spender

Requesting replacement of faulty mail order goods

Dear Sir

I am returning to you the Lovable Locket received from your firm on 13 November. The fastening on the locket is faulty, so that it will not close properly.

I should be grateful if you would send a replacement as soon as possible and also refund the postage.

Yours faithfully
Daphne Spender

Complaint about mail order goods not received

Dear Sir

Order for Poofs Inflatable Paddling Pool

On 18 January I ordered a Poofs Inflatable Paddling Pool from your company and sent a cheque for £35. According to my bank the cheque (no ...) was cashed on 28 January but my goods have not arrived.

As five weeks have now elapsed, I would be grateful if you would either send the goods within seven days of the date on this letter or refund my money.

Yours faithfully
Daphne Spender

Complaint to a newspaper advertising manager about mail order firm

Dear Sir

I am writing to complain about the Toddleoff Toy Company which has advertised regularly in your newspaper. Following the advertisement on 18 January, I ordered a Poofs Inflatable Paddling Pool, price £35.

The paddling pool did not arrive, so after allowing the 28 days stipulated for delivery, plus a further week, I wrote to the company asking for the goods or a refund within seven days. On 10 March I wrote again but I have received no answer, no goods and no refund. My bank informed me that my cheque was cashed on 28 January.

I would be grateful if you could investigate the current status of the company and let me know how I can obtain a refund.

Yours faithfully
Daphne Spender

Unsatisfactory services

Complaint to shop manager about unsatisfactory repairs

Dear Sir

On 16 August I left my Playloud radio cassette recorder at your shop for repairs to the recorder, which was unravelling and twisting every tape inserted. When I collected the machine your assistant, Mr Fibber, told me that it was now working perfectly and charged me £25.

The first time I used the machine, the tape unravelled just as before. When I returned it to your shop, Mr Fibber told me that it would cost me a further £25 to have it mended again.

As I have not received the service I paid for, I must ask that you either agree to repair the cassette player free of charge or refund my £25.

Yours faithfully
M. L. Shopper (Mrs)

Complaint to builder about shoddy work

Dear Mr Brickett

I am writing to tell you that the re-roofing work carried out by your firm at the above address is extremely unsatisfactory. On the first day of heavy rain, the new roof leaked in three places and the leaks are growing worse with each rainstorm.

Though I have telephoned several times, hoping to speak to you in person, I have always been told that you are not available. I have left urgent messages requesting you to put matters right, but you have not answered.

Unless I receive an answer from you within seven days from the date of this letter, I shall take matters further.

Yours sincerely
Arthur Household

Complaint to Trading Standards Officer about shoddy building work

Dear Sir

I hope that you will be able to take up my complaint with the Cowboy Building Company, Ranch Lane, Downtown. I enclose a copy of my letter to the head of the firm, Mr Brickett, referring to the shoddy work on the re-roofing of my house.

Mr Brickett has not answered my phone calls or my letter. I have twice called at the office in Ranch Lane but have been unable to contact anyone in authority.

Perhaps you could intercede on my behalf in this matter and make sure that the firm puts right the defects in the roof or refunds my money.

Yours faithfully
Arthur Household

Complaint to a councillor about street cleaning service

Dear Councillor Caring

I am hoping to enlist your support in persuading the local cleansing department to improve the town centre street cleaning service.

Conditions at weekends are really disgusting since the opening of Henry's Hearty Hamburgers and Chuck Chuck Fried Chicken in the High Street. By Saturday evening the gutters are thick with discarded packets, chicken bones and remnants of hamburgers. As no street cleaning takes place until Monday, the mess stays there all weekend, providing a ready meal for rats and mice.

I enclose correspondence with the cleansing department to date. As you see, the department is complacent about its current service and has no plans for substantial improvements.

I am sure that it would help a good deal if you could bring your influence to bear. Please let me know the department's response.

Yours sincerely
Elsie Anxious (Mrs)

Holidays

Complaint to the managing director of a holiday firm about a package holiday

Dear Mr Grabitall

Holiday No. D291 to Rosabella

My wife and I have just returned from two weeks' holiday at the Swindles Hotel in Rosabella.

Enclosed is a photograph taken from the balcony of our room. The empty hole surrounded by rubble is the 'large swimming pool' described in your brochure. The concrete mixer seen on the left of the picture started up promptly at 7 am every morning and the noise and dust created by the building work made it impossible to sit outside.

We complained strenuously to your resident representative, Miss Tracey Twitter, but were told that there was no alternative accommodation available at the height of the season in Rosabella.

In these circumstances, the holiday was a great disappointment, affording none of the rest and relaxation we had expected. We feel justified in claiming substantial compensation from your company and look forward to hearing your proposals.

Yours sincerely
Alan Anger

Complaint to holiday company about a package holiday, written before returning to this country

Dear Mr Grabitall

On 29 July I arrived in Rosabella, with my wife and two children, for a fortnight at the Grandiose Hotel arranged by Costalot Holidays. Instead of two rooms with sea view and balcony, as expected, we were given rooms at the side of the hotel, directly above the kitchens and with a view over a back yard with rows of dustbins. One room was small and cramped, the other was little more than a cupboard.

Over the next two days we complained several times to your representative, Miss Tracey Twitter, who told us that, due to overbooking by the hotel, there were no front rooms available and arranged to transfer us to the Modesto Hotel.

At the Modesto, we were given sea view rooms and the staff have done their best to make us comfortable. However, the hotel has none of the luxuries offered by the four-star Grandiose, and paid for as part of our holiday price. There is no swimming pool, no games room, no evening entertainment. The restaurant serves a simple, *table d'hôte* menu, rather than the wide choice of international and local dishes advertised as part of the facilities at the Grandiose.

Though we accepted the transfer as the best option available at the time, we do not consider that you have fulfilled your contract and shall be claiming a substantial refund on our return.

Yours sincerely
Alan Anger

Complaint to the managing director of a holiday company about misleading brochure claims

Dear Mr Wackiton

I wish to complain in the strongest terms about the villa holiday that I booked with your company for two adults and two children from 20 July to 2 August at Verygood Villas, Costafortune.

The chief causes for complaint are as follows:

1. The brochure describes the villas as 'beautifully situated on the outskirts of a peaceful Mediterranean village'. In fact, the village is well on the way to becoming a booming resort, with several hotels under construction, so that staying in the villas is rather like living on a building site.

2. The villas are described as being comfortably furnished. Two cane chairs with sagging seats and a couch with a considerable tilt to the left, because of a broken leg, is not a reasonable person's idea of comfort.

3. The promised daily maid service never materialized. The first week, the maid appeared twice; in the second week she came only once.

As the holiday failed to live up to the promises made in your brochure, in several important respects, I shall expect suitable recompense for the disappointment suffered by my family and myself.

Yours sincerely
Bert Brain

Complaint to the managing director of a holiday company over an offer of compensation

Dear Mr Wackiton

Your apologetic letter and offer of £30 as a 'goodwill gesture' is in no way adequate compensation for the disappointment suffered by my family and myself on the holiday provided by your firm.

As this holiday failed to live up to the promises of the brochure in several important respects, I am seeking compensation of at least one third (*or* half *or* two thirds) of the price of the holiday, which in the case of our family was £...

Yours sincerely
Bert Brain

Follow-up letter, if the answer is still unsatisfactory

Dear Mr Wackiton

I have received your letter dated 4 September, offering the derisory amount of £75 in compensation for my family's disastrous holiday.

This is, of course, unacceptable and if a satisfactory settlement is not forthcoming within seven days of the date of this letter, I shall be forced to pursue the matter through the Association of British Travel Agents (*or* I shall be forced to take legal action).

Yours sincerely
Bert Brain

Council and government departments

Complaint to the Director of Social Services about a decision on home help

Dear Mrs Heart

Three weeks ago social services informed my mother that she did not qualify for a home help.

At first, I thought this must be an administrative error but it has since been confirmed by the department and I have been unable to persuade them to change their minds. I am told that because my mother is 'not totally housebound', no home help can be provided.

I would point out that my mother is 80 years old, lives alone and has an arthritic hip. She leaves the house only when absolutely necessary to buy food or collect a prescription from the chemist because she is too independent to ask neighbours for help.

Whenever she leaves the house she is in danger of falling and injuring herself and if she had the services of a home help she would no longer have to take these risks.

I hope that you will be able to persuade the department concerned to reconsider my mother's case.

Yours sincerely
Alan Anger

Complaint to the council about rubbish collection

Dear Sirs

I wish to draw your attention to the deteriorating standard of rubbish collection in the district.

My dustbin has remained unemptied for three weeks out of the last six. Neighbours tell me that they have experienced the same problem. Sometimes the dustmen ignore two or three houses in a row, sometimes a single house is missed. Every visit by the dustmen means a trail of rubbish strewn over gardens and down the roadway. Bin lids are thrown carelessly on the ground to blow about in the wind.

Please let me know what action you propose to take to improve this service.

Yours faithfully
Arthur Houseman

Complaint to the Environmental Health Department about a dangerous dog

Dear Sir

I am writing to complain about a vicious dog belonging to Mr Robert Growler of 17, Barking Road, Portsend. The dog, a large mongrel, is allowed to roam the streets freely, frightening local children and terrorizing pets.

Yesterday he bounded across the road to chase my 10-year-old daughter and managed to tear a piece out of her dress as she reached her doorstep. Next time, his teeth may well fasten in her leg, rather than her clothes.

Like me, my neighbours all carry umbrellas when walking down the road, as the dog frequently comes snapping and snarling at our heels. I understand that the postman refuses to deliver to Mr Growler's house and the milkman leaves bottles at the end of the drive.

Several residents of Barking Road have asked Mr Growler to restrain his dog but he remains deaf to our requests. Therefore I hope we can rely on your assistance in this matter.

Yours faithfully
Elsie Anxious (Mrs)

Complaint to the Environmental Health Department about noise

Dear Sir

I am writing to ask you to take action to stop the unreasonable night-time noise caused by the occupants of No. 6, Popround Crescent.

Several young people moved in to share the house four weeks ago and since then stereo music has blared out every evening, seldom stopping before 3 am. All the doors and windows remain open and numbers of people wander about the garden and the street, singing and shouting. None of the neighbours, including a couple aged 80 and several young children, are able to sleep while this goes on.

At least four of the residents of Popround Crescent have tried to make polite complaints but we have been met with abusive language and obscene gestures and we have been unable to discover the name of the householder.

I attach a list of names of residents who are prepared to join me in my complaint and hope that you will use your good offices to stop this nuisance.

Yours faithfully
Elsie Anxious (Mrs)

Complaint to Trading Standards Department about dangerous toys

Dear Sir

I recently bought a toy fire engine for my five-year-old nephew from Kiddyfun at 112, High Street. Within a few days, one of the wheels came off, leaving an unguarded sharp spike projecting from the body of the toy. Fortunately the child's mother was there at the time, so no accident resulted.

The manager of Kiddyfun refunded my money and promised to withdraw the engines, which are manufactured by Cheapo Ltd, from sale. However, I feel that the matter needs further investigation, as other shops in the area are still selling these potentially dangerous toys.

Yours faithfully
M. L. Shopper

Complaint to the council about hygiene in parks

Dear Sir

I must draw your attention to the filthy state of Downtown Park.

Litter baskets are emptied so seldom that they are usually overflowing, with piles of paper and food remnants around the base. Cans and broken bottles litter the grass, making it unsafe for children to play.

Please let me know what measures you propose to take to remedy this state of affairs. The park is, after all, one of the local amenities and as such, we all pay for it.

Yours faithfully
Anne Walker

Complaint to the Highways Department about a dangerous crossing

Dear Sir

Urgent action is needed over the crossing at the junction of Dewpond Road and Cobblers Road.

This is a T junction with traffic lights and these have no pedestrian signals, so that pedestrians have to hasten across in the few seconds between one line of traffic stopping and the next line starting off.

Since the new shopping precinct opened, on the far side of Dewpond Road, this has become a serious hazard as many more pedestrians use this crossing every day. As the traffic here is busy and fast-moving, they often find themselves running for their lives.

Please could I ask you to install pedestrian crossing lights in the immediate future, before someone is seriously injured.

Yours faithfully
Anne Walker

Writing to an MP, taking the matter of a dangerous crossing further

Dear Mrs Westminster

I am writing to ask you to intercede with the Highways Department of Downtown Council who are unwilling to take action over a dangerous road crossing.

The junction of Dewpond Road and Cobblers Road is used constantly by pedestrians, since the building of the new shopping precinct, yet there is no pedestrian light and they frequently have to sprint across the road, bags of shopping in both hands, to avoid fast-moving traffic.

As you will see from the attached correspondence, I have been pressing the Highways Department to install pedestrian crossing lights for three months without success. I even sent the names of forty-three shoppers – which I collected in two hours – supporting my request.

Could you please exert some pressure on them to take action? Surely we should not have to wait for a death or serious accident before they see sense.

Yours sincerely
Anne Walker

5

Home Finance

Brevity and clarity are essential for any letters dealing with financial matters. Keep your statements crisp and factual and make sure you leave no room for misunderstanding. Once you have written the letter, check carefully to ensure that you have included all the relevant facts. Quote your account number when dealing with the bank, your policy number when writing to an insurance company and so on. Keep a copy of your letter and if you need to enclose documents, send copies, not originals.

Business with banks and insurance companies can often be transacted by filling in a form, which will detail all the information needed, but you may still want to write a letter to explain your particular circumstances. This could be useful if, for instance, you are applying for a loan and feel that, because you will be going back to work as soon as the children start school in September or because you are expecting some money from your grandmother's estate within a couple of months, you are a better risk than would be indicated by the facts on the form.

If you get into difficulties over finance and find that you are unable to pay your mortgage or your bills it is important to write promptly to your creditors, explaining the situation and asking for time to pay or proposing reduced payments. Most organizations will be understanding, so long as you keep them informed and show you are making efforts to sort it out.

Banks

Querying a bank statement

Dear Sir
<u>Account No. .....</u>

I note from my current statement that my monthly standing order of £5 to the Alliance of Workers and Shirkers was paid twice in May.

Would you please rectify this and see that the amount overpaid is credited to my account.

Yours faithfully
Cynthia Smart

Asking for an appointment with the bank manager

Dear Sir

I have recently received a legacy of £40,000 and would like your advice on where to invest the money to give a reasonable return with the minimum of risk.

Perhaps I could come and discuss investment possibilities with you one day next week. A time between 12 pm and 2 pm would be convenient for me, as I can fit this in with my lunch hour.

Yours faithfully
Gerald Goodbody

Asking a bank manager to stop a cheque

Dear Sir

Account number ....

I am writing to confirm my telephone call asking you to stop payment on cheque number .... for the amount of £25. This was dated 22 December and made out to Miss Doreen Duckitt.

This cheque, sent through the post, failed to arrive and I am about to issue a replacement.

Yours faithfully
Louise Percy (Mrs)

Instructing a bank to pay a standing order

Dear Sir

Account number ....

Please pay a standing order for the amount of £10 to the Furry Feline Friends Rescue Fund beginning on 1 May, then on the same date of each month, until further notice.

The FFFRF account is at Goldbags Bank, account number ....

Yours faithfully
Pamela Puss (Miss)

Instructing a bank to cancel a standing order

Dear Sir

<u>Account number ....</u>

Please cancel my six monthly standing order to the Alliance of Workers and Shirkers immediately. The last payment was made on 30 January 19—.

Yours faithfully
Christian Clutter

Asking a bank manager to open an account for a school leaver

Dear Mr Thrift

<u>Account number ....</u>

My daughter Sujun is leaving school in two weeks' time and starting her first job as a clerk with Broom and Sweep. She would like to open an account with Moneybags Bank, where I have been banking for the past 15 years.

I would be grateful if you would make the necessary arrangements and I will ask Sujun to call in one lunch hour next week to complete any necessary paperwork.

Yours sincerely
Kenneth Wong

Asking for a replacement autobank card

Dear Sir

<u>Autobank card number ...</u>

When I attempted to withdraw my money from the bank cash dispenser yesterday evening, the machine told me that I had entered an incorrect number and 'confiscated' my card. This is the second time that this has happened in the past month.

As I am using the correct personal identification number, I think that the card must be faulty, so I would ask you to issue a new card without delay.

Yours faithfully
James Jinx

Requesting an overdraft

Dear Mr Thrift

Account number ....

I have recently set up my own business as a management consultant and this has made my cash flow position difficult, on a purely temporary basis.

Would it be possible to arrange overdraft facilities for me up to a limit of £... per month? I will probably need this facility for 12 months.

Please let me know whether there is a fee for this service and how much interest will be charged.

Yours sincerely
Toby Trott

Explaining an unauthorized overdraft

Dear Mr Thrift

Thank you for your letter dated 18 May, drawing my attention to my overdraft of £....

This was due to an oversight. I had not realized that there was insufficient cash in the account to cover a large cheque paid to Brick and Mortar Ltd for building materials needed to complete a contract.

I am expecting a substantial payment from a customer within the next couple of days and I shall therefore be able to clear the overdraft by the end of the week.

Yours sincerely
Barry Bodgett

Requesting a loan

Dear Sir

Account number ...

I wish to apply for a personal loan of £... , needed for a loft conversion to my house. I already have £... towards the estimated cost of £...

As you will see from your records, I have always kept my current account in credit though for the past three years my income has been variable, coming from freelance assignments.

However, from 10 September I begin work as senior editor with Health Nuts Publishers at a salary of £... a month. I attach a calculation of my monthly disposable income and from this you will see that I can easily afford repayments of £... a month. I would expect to repay the full amount of the loan within a period of two years.

Yours faithfully
Arthur Houseman

Enc.

Asking the bank to act as executor for a will

Dear Sir

I wish to appoint Moneybags Bank as the executor of my will. Please send me details of your fees for this service.

Yours faithfully
Colin Careful

Insurance companies

Arranging insurance for a house removal

Dear Sir

Policy number .....

I am planning to move house on 4 July. Please let me know what arrangements you can make for extending my existing contents policy to cover removal risks and what additional premium will be payable.

Please specify whether or not the removal insurance will cover damage by scratching, denting or tearing.

Yours faithfully
Gerald Goodbody

Notifying the company of a claim following a removal

Dear Sir

Policy number ...

As you have specified that a claim under my removal insurance must be notified within 48 hours of the move, I write to tell you of my intention to make a claim.

70

So far, I have identified the following damage:

1. The glass in the grandfather clock is broken
2. A corner has been knocked off a carved bookcase
3. One table lamp is broken
4. The back of the settee has been badly torn

I am still checking through my possessions and shall contact you with full details in the near future.

Yours faithfully
Gerald Goodbody

Adding to all risks insurance

Dear Sir

Policy number ....

Please add the following item to the specified items covered by my all risks policy:

1 XYZ computer, value £1,700

I attach a copy of the sales receipt. Please let me know if any additional premium is payable.

Yours faithfully
Christopher Crisp

Enc.

Notifying insurers of a neighbour's claim against you

Dear Sir

Claim number .../Policy number ...

Following the fire at my house on 24 February, for which I have already made a claim, I have received a letter from my neighbour claiming for damage to his property caused by the fire. I enclose a copy of the letter.

I have told my neighbour that I am unable to negotiate with him direct and that I have put the matter in your hands.

Yours faithfully
Edward Eccleston

Enc.

Adding further losses to a claim made after a burglary

Dear Sir

Claim number .../Policy number ...

When I filled in my claim form for the burglary at my house on the night of 6 October, I included all the losses known at that time. Since then, my family has discovered the loss of further objects at the time of the burglary. These are:

1. One personal stereo, bought three weeks ago, value £50
2. One gold bracelet, value approx. £60
3. One portable typewriter, three years old, approx. value £60

Please add these items to my claim.

Yours faithfully
Terence Tutley-Brown

Negotiating with insurers over stolen items recovered

Dear Sir

Claim number .../Policy number ....

The police have informed me that some of the items stolen from my house on 24 June last year have been recovered.

Among these is my wife's diamond and ruby engagement ring, which was valued at £250. As you can imagine, this is of great sentimental value and we would like to have it back.

As our claim was met in full by your company, we should like to arrange to pay back the amount covering the ring and regain this item. Please let me know if this is agreeable to you.

Yours faithfully
Percy Philpott

Enquiring about reductions in motor insurance premiums

Dear Sir

Policy number ...

On 13 November I shall be moving from the above London address to The Brackens, Heath Road, Countrytown, Wiltshire WP4 2AL. All other policy details are unchanged.

Please let me know what adjustment will be made in my motor insurance premium for this change from city to rural area.

Yours faithfully
Martin Mole

Changing the basis of motor insurance

Dear Sir

<u>Policy number ...</u>

I wish to reduce my insurance from comprehensive to third party, fire and theft, with immediate effect.

Please arrange for the alteration to my policy or, if necessary, send me a new proposal form.

Yours faithfully
Henry Hubble

Asking for an excess on a motor policy

Dear Sir

<u>Policy number ...</u>

I have received my renewal notice for the above policy and, because of the considerable increase, I would like to reduce my premiums by accepting a voluntary excess.

Please let me know how an excess of £50 would affect my premium.

Yours faithfully
Noreen Nurse (Miss)

Reporting an accident when no claim is to be made

Dear Sir

<u>Policy number ...</u>

On 15 February I was involved in a collision with Mrs Betty Bumper of 65 Crashing Lane, Downtown. Both vehicles suffered minor damage but no-one was injured.

As you require notification of any accident, I enclose a completed accident report form. However, I do not wish to claim under my policy and prefer to deal with the matter myself.

Yours faithfully
Charles Bachelor

Enc.

Cancelling motor insurance

Dear Sir

<u>Policy number ...</u>

I wish to cancel the above policy with effect from today as my car has now been sold for scrap. I enclose my insurance certificate and should be grateful if you would forward a cheque to cover the unexpired time on my premium.

Yours faithfully
Clint Cocky

Enc.

Notifying insurers of the theft of a car

Dear Sir

<u>Policy number ...</u>

I am writing to inform you that my car was stolen on the evening of 26 May, from the car park behind the Galaxy Cinema, Portsend. The theft was reported to Highgrove Road police station.

I realize that no payment for loss can be made for some weeks. If the car is recovered within this time I shall let you know immediately.

Yours faithfully
Sybil Swift (Mrs)

Credit

Confirming notification of the loss of a credit card

Dear Sir

I am writing to confirm my telephone call to your office this morning, notifying you of the loss of my credit card, number ....

The card was in my purse when it was stolen in Downtown High Street. As I rang within 30 minutes of the theft, I trust that you will be able to take action to prevent its unauthorized use.

Yours faithfully
Pamela Perky (Miss)

Querying an item on a credit card statement

Dear Sir

Account number ...

I have just received my Spendit card statement dated 3 August. Among the list of payments is an item of £26.35 paid to Bliss Boutique on 26 July, reference number ....

As I have made no purchases from this shop, I believe that I have been charged in error. Would you please check your records for more details and let me know the outcome?

Yours faithfully
Sidney Shopper

Querying interest charged on a credit card statement

Dear Sir

Account number ....

I have just received my Spendit card statement dated 3 August. On this you have listed a balance of £35.50 carried over from last month, with interest charged.

If you check your records you will find that I paid this amount over the counter at Moneybags Bank four clear working days before the date on which payment was due. Attached is a copy of the receipt.

I enclose a cheque for £28.35. This is the balance outstanding on the current month, after subtracting last month's balance from the statement.

Yours faithfully
Sidney Shopper

Enc.

Asking for extra time to pay debts

Dear Sirs

Agreement number ...

I am having difficulty in meeting the payments on my Sizzle-Up cooker, Mark II, purchased in January 19— and am writing to ask you to accept reduced payments for the time being.

Over the first six months, all payments were made on time but since then I have been away from work with a back injury. As my income depends largely on commission and bonuses, the basic pay I have been receiving is not sufficient to cover my regular outgoings.

I wish to offer to pay off my debt at the rate of £20 a month until my circumstances improve, when I will make arrangements to clear the outstanding amount more quickly.

Yours faithfully
Samuel Strapped

Second request for extra time to pay debts

Dear Sirs

Agreement number...

Thank you for your letter dated 10 June. I was sorry that you did not feel able to accept my offer of repayments at the rate of £20 a month.

I hope that, in the light of further information, you might reconsider. Attached is a full statement of my income and regular outgoings and a list of creditors and the amounts I have offered to pay. As you see, Spendit Credit Cards, Toogood Stores and Ferret Finance have already agreed to my proposals.

I am keen to pay off all my debts and I feel that it would be more satisfactory for you to receive payment in full over a longer period than first agreed, rather than to repossess a second hand cooker.

Yours faithfully
Samuel Strapped

Enc.

Mortgages

Notifying lenders about problems in keeping up payments

Dear Sir

Mortgage account number ...

I am having great difficulty in meeting my mortgage payments at the moment. I have been out of work for the past four months, since the closure of Reckless and Quick Ltd.

If possible, I would like to arrange to pay interest only on my mortgage for a short period, say six months, in which time I hope to resolve my present difficulties.

As you know, new industries are moving into the area and should be recruiting in the autumn, so I have high hopes of new employment at that time.

Yours faithfully
Lawrence Luckless

OR

Dear Sir

<u>Mortgage account number ...</u>

I write to ask if it would be possible to extend the period of my mortgage from 25 to 30 years. I lost my job as works manager with Buckett and Sludge Ltd six months ago, because of large scale cutbacks within the firm.

I have now accepted a new job with Box and Cox but this has meant a salary reduction from £... to £... Therefore it is necessary to arrange a permanent reduction in my regular outgoings.

Please let me know if you are willing to arrange this.

Yours faithfully
Harold Hapless

Enquiring about repaying a mortgage

Dear Sir

<u>Mortgage account number...</u>

I am considering paying off the remaining amount of my mortgage in a lump sum. Please let me know how much is outstanding and whether or not you will make any charge if I decide to repay immediately.

Yours faithfully
Mohammed Naziv

Applying for an extra loan

Dear Sir

Mortgage account number ...

I need to finance improvement work on my house and wish to apply for an extra loan on top of my mortgage. The work involves complete rewiring and the enlargement of an inadequate bathroom.

The local authority has agreed to an improvement grant to cover 60 per cent of the cost. As you will see from the enclosed statement, this still leaves the outstanding amount of £...

Since I took the original loan, my income has risen from £... to £... per annum, so I would have no difficulty in meeting the additional payments.

If an extra loan is a possibility, please let me know what legal and administrative fees would be involved.

Yours faithfully
Gary Gore-Brown

Tax

Appealing against an assessment

Dear Sir

Assessment number ...

I have checked the notice of assessment for the year ending April 4 19— but I do not agree with your figures.

It seems that you have credited me with a single person's allowance rather than a married man's allowance. You will see from your records that I notified you of my marriage on June 6 19—.

I would be grateful if you would check your figures and adjust as necessary.

Yours faithfully
Henry Husband

Notifying tax inspectors of a change in status

Dear Sir

Please note that on 31 March 19— I left my job with Spanner and Pipe Ltd and I am now a self-employed plumber. From that date I apply for taxation under Schedule D.

Yours faithfully
Walter Wrench

Explaining a mistake in tax returns

Dear Sir

Thank you for your letter dated 17 May in which you said that you had reason to believe that I had not disclosed the full amount of my earnings in the tax year ending 4 April 19—.

On checking my records I find that I omitted a single payment of £250 from Shuffle and Plodd from my calculations.

This was an oversight on my part and, to my knowledge, there are no other undisclosed payments.

Yours faithfully
Tony Twister

Miscellaneous

Asking a solicitor to add a codicil to a will

Dear Mr Foggett

I wish to add a further bequest to my will, drawn up by you in March 19—.

Please prepare a codicil leaving £2000 to the Furry Feline Friends Rescue Service and send it to me for signature.

Yours sincerely
Pamela Puss

Withdrawing money from a building society account

Dear Sir

<u>Account number....</u>

I am writing to give the required one month's notice of my intention to withdraw £.... from my account. My pass book is enclosed.

Yours faithfully
Norman Nipper

Enc.

Approaching the Home Improvements Officer of the local council about grants

Dear Sir

I wish to bring my property up to a good standard by major work on the roof and floors and I would be grateful if you could tell me if I would be eligible for a grant from the council. This is a terraced house built in 1902 and I am an owner occupier.

Please send details of the type of grant I should apply for and the eligible expense limits on such a grant.

Yours faithfully
Percy Pickett

Enquiring about income support

Dear Sir

I have recently separated from my husband and as my income is only £— a week and I have no savings, I believe I qualify for income support.

Would you please send me the appropriate claim form.

Yours faithfully
Helga Hardup

Writing in response to a demand for payment for television licence

Dear Sir

I have received a second demand for payment of a television licence for the above address.

I have not paid the licence fee because I do not own a television set. I have never owned a television set and have no plans to install one in the future.

Please amend your records accordingly and send no further demands.

Yours faithfully
Roger Righteous

Querying a telephone bill with telephone company

Dear Sir

<u>Your ref ...</u>

I have received my telephone bill dated 3 July and find the amount of £130 inexplicably high.

The charges for previous quarters have been steady at between £60 and £75. During the latest quarter only my wife and I have had access to the telephone. We have made no more calls than usual and were away on holiday for three weeks during this period.

I would be grateful if you could check your records for possible mistakes and let me know the result.

Yours faithfully
Albert Anxious

6

Employment

It is worth taking a good deal of trouble over a letter of application. This is the first contact you have with a prospective employer and if he is unimpressed, you may never have the chance to put across your personality and capability at an interview. The immediate impression given by your letter can be important, so use good quality paper and set out your letter carefully, so that it is centred on the paper, well spaced and with no great white spaces top or bottom.

Typing is usually best, though some firms ask for handwritten applications. This may mean that the job requires legible handwriting, so take as much time as you need to produce a neat, readable script with a clear signature, rather than an illegible squiggle. Whether you write or type, read the letter carefully when you have finished and if you find the smallest mistake, begin again.

Your letter should be long enough to mention the main points of your suitability for the particular job on offer and no more; never allow yourself to ramble. You should come over as keen and positive without sounding too full of yourself. Make sure that you do everything the advertisement asks. If it says 'state age', then do so, even if you would rather conceal the fact that you are only 20 or already over 50. If you are asked to 'state salary required', then you must give your best estimate, even though you would prefer to hear what they are offering first. Many firms will simply discard letters that do not give the facts requested, without looking further.

You do not have to refer to your reasons for wanting to leave your present job but if you do, never criticize your employers or imply that you are under-valued or under-paid. Refer instead to the extra scope and responsibility of the new post and its opportunity for using extra skills or widening your horizons.

The tone of your letter may depend on the type of firm involved. Obviously you could use a brighter, more individual style if you were applying to an up-and-coming advertising agency or a trendy fashion house than if you were applying to a staid family law firm or an old-established gents' outfitters.

Never attempt to give your full work history in a letter. Instead attach a *curriculum vitae*, securely stapled to your letter. This should contain basic information such as your name, address, home and work phone numbers, date of birth, educational qualifications and details of positions held, with dates. Your *curriculum vitae* will be more eye-catching if you list your present job first, then work backwards in time to your beginnings. Make sure that you give a clear idea of what your present job involves: your responsibilities, the field covered, how many people report to you.

Letters such as those offering jobs, accepting or rejecting offers and resigning all follow accepted patterns but references can be a little more tricky. The convention is that you are as encouraging as possible about former pupils or employees when writing a reference but you should never be deliberately misleading. Employers are adept at reading between the lines and they know that anyone summed up as 'accurate and trustworthy' is probably a plodder while 'capable of flashes of brilliance' means able but unreliable.

Applying for a job

Requesting a job application form

Dear Sir

I am interested in your advertisement in the Portsend Post for an assistant bursar and would be grateful if you would send me an application form and job description for this post.

Yours faithfully
Simon Scrooge

Application for a first job

Dear Mr Pullon

I understand that you are looking for a reliable young person to train as a dental nurse and I write to ask if you would consider me for this position.

On 20 July I shall be leaving Canon Carr Comprehensive, after taking five GCSE subjects: English, Maths, Biology, Environmental Studies and Home Economics.

During my last year I have been a school prefect and captain of the netball team.

I am looking for a job involving personal responsibility and dealing with people. I attach a reference written by my head teacher, Mr Rule.

Yours sincerely
Tracey Tripp

Speculative application to an expanding firm

Dear Sirs

I was interested in your recent advertisement for food technologists and sales and marketing staff. As this indicates that your company is expanding at the moment, I write to ask if you have any openings for an experienced dietician.

I enclose a *curriculum vitae* from which you will see that I have experience directly relevant to the scope of your company and I think I would be able to make a useful contribution.

Though I realize that you may have no immediate vacancies in this area, I would be grateful if you would keep my letter on file and contact me if any opportunities occur in the near future.

Yours faithfully
Lettice Nutting

Speculative application by an employee about to be made redundant

Dear Sir

For the past 18 months I have been working as a designer for Mod Modes but, following the takeover by Debby Dresses, the contraction in the ready-to-wear side of the firm's business means that my post will be redundant in three months' time.

I am interested in your company because I have seen how imaginative and forward-looking your approach to the market has been over the past few years and wonder if there might be any vacancies in the near future for someone with my background and experience, plus a great deal of enthusiasm.

I would be grateful for the opportunity of showing you some examples of my work and discussing the possibilities with you.

Yours faithfully
Dee Darnley-Smith

Application for a job as a trainee VDU operator

Dear Sir

Trainee VDU operator

I wish to apply for the job advertised in today's Portsend Post.

I am 18 years old and have 'O' levels in English and Maths and CSEs in Technical Drawing, Computer Studies, Geography and Biology.

On leaving Alderman Carter Comprehensive in July 1988, I spent six months as a counter hand at Henry's Hearty Hamburgers and since then I have been employed as an office junior with Bodge and Blowitt, Building Contractors.

Though this has given me a useful training in the basic working of a busy office, I am keen to find an opportunity to learn about computers.

I should be pleased to attend an interview at any time.

Yours faithfully
Holly Hopeful

Applying for a job as a nanny

Dear Madam

I wish to apply for the job as nanny advertised in the March issue of Toddlers' World Monthly.

I hold the National Nursery Examination Board certificate, gained after a two year course at Portsend College of Further Education and for the past two and a half years I have been employed as nanny for two children, aged seven and five.

In my present job I am often left in sole charge when my employers, Mr and Mrs Bunce, are abroad on business. I am 21 years old and am a competent driver with a clean licence.

Mr Bunce has accepted an overseas posting and this is the reason that I am seeking another job. My employers are willing to give me a good reference and are happy for you to contact them by letter or telephone.

Yours faithfully
Noreen Nurse

Applying for a job as an electrician

Dear Sir

I am writing in response to your advertisement in the Carberry Courier for a skilled electrician and would like to apply for the post.

Since completing my apprenticeship with Plugs and Sparks Electrics four years ago, I have been working as Approved Electrician responsible to the foreman for industrial, commercial and domestic installations and for training two apprentices.

I am fully experienced in the installation and maintenance of air conditioning systems, fire alarms and smoke detection equipment and I am used to working from plans and drawings without direct supervision.

I shall be glad to supply references.

Yours faithfully
Rana Kabeer

Applying for a job as a personal assistant

Dear Mr Big

Personal assistant to director

I was interested to read your advertisement in the Downtown Post of 5 June and would like to apply for the position.

As you will see from the enclosed *curriculum vitae*, I have been employed as personal secretary to the Managing Director of Growbig Exports Ltd for the past three years.

In this post I have been used to interviewing callers, drafting letters for signature, preparing agendas for meetings, taking verbatim notes and editing minutes, as well as supervising two junior secretaries.

My shorthand speed is 120 wpm, my typing speed is 60 wpm and I am familiar with computer keyboard operation.

I am now 28 years old and though I have been very happy with my present employers, I am seeking promotion and an opportunity to develop my skills further.

Yours faithfully
Hannah Hubble (Miss)

Applying for a job as retail sales manager

Dear Mr Pushitt

<u>Retail sales manager</u>

I would like to apply for the position advertised in the Carberry Courier on 17 April.

As you will see from the enclosed *curriculum vitae*, I have worked for Toogood Stores for 12 years, progressing from sales assistant to branch manager. I now manage the Carberry High Street branch where I am responsible for recruiting and supervising 21 members of staff.

The store was acquired in the merger between Toogood Stores and Homeshops and when I took over as manager in 19—, my brief was to reorganize and revive a flagging business. Within the first year the volume of sales increased by 60 per cent and in the two years since my appointment has risen by 90 per cent.

At the moment I am looking for an opportunity to take on a new challenge, such as the post you advertize.

Yours sincerely
David Doe

Curriculum vitae for a job as retail sales manager

C U R R I C U L U M   V I T A E

D A V I D   D O E

The Falcons, Manor Road, Carberry CV4 9LS

Telephone: 456 6789 (home); 234 5678 (business)

Date of birth: 22 June 19—

EXPERIENCE

March 19— to date
Branch manager, Toogood Stores, Carberry High Street, Carberry
Responsible for the profitable operation of a 745 square metre retail
shop and the recruitment, training and supervision of an assistant
manager and 20 sales assistants.

January 19— to March 19—
Assistant manager, Toogood Stores, Portsend
Responsible to manager for day-to-day running of a 835 square metre
retail shop, including performance of sales staff.

October 19— to January 19—
Departmental manager, lingerie department, Toogood Stores, Oxford
Street, London

May 19— to October 19—
Section manager, beauty department, Toogood Stores, Oxford Street,
London

January 19— to May 19—
Junior management trainee, Toogood Stores, Oxford Street, London
Job rotation training including distribution, dispatch, personnel and
accounts as well as work on the shop floor.

September 19— to January 19—
Sales assistant, Toogood Stores, Oxford Street, London

EDUCATION

September 19— to July 19—, David Dalrymple Comprehensive
School, Roundabout, London SW10

June 19— 4 GCE 'O' Levels: English Language, English Literature,
Mathematics, Home Economics

References

Asking for a reference from a teacher

Dear Mr Wise,

I am applying for the post of trainee chef at Stuffs Restaurant and, following an interview, I have been asked to supply two letters of reference.

Would you be willing to act as a referee for me? I should be most grateful if you feel that you could recommend me as a promising employee.

I enclose a stamped addressed envelope.

Yours sincerely,
Errol Carson

Asking a family friend to act as a referee

Dear Mr Glendenning,

I shall be coming down from university in July and I am applying for jobs in the computer field. I am writing to ask if I may use your name as a referee.

As a long-standing friend of the family, I'm sure you have a shrewd idea of my capabilities and I know that anything you feel able to say in my favour would carry weight with a prospective employer.

Yours,
Wayne Wagstaff

Asking a previous employer for a reference

Dear Mr Smith

I am applying for a post as purchasing manager with Crimp and Crump and I am hoping that you would be willing to stand as a referee, along with my current employer. I enclose a copy of the job advertisement, which gives an idea of what the post entails.

I still have very happy memories of my time with your company and I send my best wishes to you and to all those who still remember me.

Yours sincerely
Richard Yip

Taking up a reference

Dear Mr Dobbin

We are considering Miss Constance Cash for the position of company accountant. This position entails budgeting and forecasting, supervising the day-to-day running of the office and the ability to work to tight deadlines in a pressurized environment.

Miss Cash has given your name as a reference, as I understand that she is currently employed by you in a similar capacity.

I would be grateful for your opinion, in the strictest confidence, of her ability and efficiency.

Yours sincerely
Peter Pushitt

Providing a reference for an able employee

Dear Mr Pushitt

I am very happy to recommend Miss Cash. She is reliable, efficient and energetic. She handles pressure with cool competence and has a pleasant manner that smooths over difficult situations.

We shall be sorry to lose her but I have known for some time that she was looking for a post with a larger organization.

Yours sincerely
David Dobbin

Providing a less enthusiastic reference

Dear Mr Sparks

Mr Patrick Plodd has been employed by us for two years as a motor mechanic. His work under supervision is competent and he is well-liked in the workshop.

Yours sincerely
Clifford Carman

Providing a reference for a school leaver

Dear Mr Pullon

Tracey Tripp has attended Canon Carr Comprehensive from September 1985 to July 1990 and during that time she has always been hardworking and determined to succeed in anything she attempted. Her attendance record is good and she has a pleasant personality.

In her year as a prefect she has shown that she is able to take responsibility and cope with situations on her own initiative.

Yours sincerely
Reginald Rule

Refusing a reference

Dear Mr Murgatroyd

I regret that I am unable to provide a reference for Mrs Cherry Crook. When she left our firm I informed her that no reference would be forthcoming. Under the circumstances, I prefer to say no more.

Yours sincerely
Herbert Honest

Providing a reference for a daily help

Dear Mrs Household

Mrs Moppit has worked for a me as a daily help for the past two years and has always been cheerful, reliable and trustworthy.

She is only leaving us because she finds the journey difficult.

Yours sincerely
Margaret Green

Dealing with applications

Rejecting a speculative application

Dear Miss Perky

Thank you for your letter of 6 September expressing an interest in working for this company.

I am sorry to say that we have no vacancies at present and have no reason to think that any suitable opening will occur in the immediate future.

Yours sincerely
Basil Blower

Rejecting a speculative application but expressing interest

Dear Miss Perky

Thank you for your letter of 6 September asking about job opportunities within the company.

Unfortunately we have no suitable vacancies at present but I was interested to read of your wide experience and would like to keep your letter on file. If an opening does occur within the near future, I shall contact you without delay.

With all good wishes,

Yours sincerely
Basil Blower

Rejecting a job application in reply to an advertisement

Dear Mr Cocky

Thank you for your application for the post of sales manager.

We have received a large number of applicants and have been forced to confine our interviews to those with the most relevant experience.

Therefore I regret that we are not able to consider you for the position.

Yours sincerely
Kenneth Killjoy

Acknowledging a job application and putting it on 'hold'

Dear Miss Philpott

Thank you for your application for the post of assistant personnel manager within this company.

We have had a very heavy response to our advertisement and it will take some time to consider them in detail and decide on a short list for interview.

I hope that we shall be in a position to contact you again within a fortnight.

Yours sincerely
Matthew Murgatroyd

Inviting an applicant for an interview

Dear Miss Philpott

As promised in my letter of 10 March, I now write to tell you that we have considered all the applications for the post of personnel manager and would like to invite you for a preliminary interview.

Please telephone my secretary Miss Pursell on extension 54, to arrange a convenient time. We will, of course, reimburse your travel expenses.

I look forward to seeing you.

Yours sincerely
Matthew Murgatroyd

Rejecting a job application after an interview

Dear Miss Philpott

We have now completed our review of applicants and I am sorry to say that we are unable to offer you the position of personnel manager.

I should like to thank you for your interest and for your time in attending the interview.

With very best wishes for your success in the future,

Yours sincerely
Matthew Murgatroyd.

Job offers

Offering a job

Dear Mrs Swift

Following our meeting on 8 May, I am very pleased to be able to offer you the appointment as marketing executive, beginning on 1 October. The initial salary is £....., to be reviewed after six months.

Please sign the enclosed contract of employment and return it to me as soon as possible.

I look forward to welcoming you to the company and hope that you will enjoy working for us.

Yours sincerely
Johnson Lai

Accepting a job offer

Dear Mr Pushitt

Thank you for your letter dated 20 September.

I am very pleased to accept your offer of a post as secretary to the works manager. I have signed the contract of employment, which I return with this letter.

I look forward to working for you and shall be pleased to report to the Personnel Department at 9 am on 30 September.

Yours sincerely
Prunella Prim

OR

Dear Mr Pushitt

Thank you very much for your letter of 20 September offering me the position of secretary to the marketing director.

I note the conditions of service set out in your letter and that my salary will be £....., subject to review in six months.

I look forward to joining your company on 30 September.

Yours sincerely
Priscilla Prim

Refusing a job offer

Dear Mr Pushitt

Thank you very much for your letter dated 20 September offering me the post of assistant personnel officer. However, I regret that I am unable to accept.

Since our meeting, my company has made me a very attractive offer and, under the circumstances, I have decided to stay with them.

Yours sincerely
Colin Clinch

OR

Dear Mr Pushitt

Thank you very much for your letter dated 20 September offering me the post of administrative assistant.

I am grateful for your confidence in me but I have to decline your offer as I accepted a post with Stutter and Tripp several days before I received your letter.

Yours sincerely
Frances Figgins

Resignations

Resigning after the offer of a new job

Dear Mr Murgatroyd

I have accepted a position as works foreman with Box and Cox Ltd and must therefore give four weeks notice of my intention to leave the company on February 28.

As you will understand, this post is an important career step for me and I am looking forward to tackling new responsibilities.

However, I shall be sorry to leave Bell and Clapper. My three years here have been very happy and I am sure that the experience I have gained will stand me in good stead in the future.

Yours sincerely
Brian Bush

Resigning after problems in the firm

Dear Mr Pushitt

As you know, I have been out of sympathy with the policy of the company since the merger last July. This has meant increasing tension within the department and I feel that I must offer my resignation.

I am sure you will agree that it is not desirable for me to work out my three months notice. I should like to leave as soon as possible and hope that we can agree on a mutually satisfactory date.

Yours sincerely
Alan Anger

Accepting a resignation

Dear Mrs Gorringe

Thank you for your letter of 4 May resigning from your position with the company.

I am sorry to hear that you are leaving us but I am sure that your promotion is well deserved and hope that it will bring you both success and satisfaction.

Yours sincerely
Michael Messenger

Staff

Explaining absence on grounds of illness

Dear Mr Grinder

As my wife explained on the telephone yesterday, I have a throat infection which has prevented me from coming to work. The doctor called this morning and told me that I must stay in bed for the rest of the week. I enclose a certificate.

I hope that I shall have recovered by next Monday but if not I will, of course, let you know.

Yours sincerely
Humphrey Kibblewhite

Explaining absence on compassionate grounds

Dear Mr Grinder

As I explained to your secretary on the telephone, I had to hurry down to Worthing this morning, as my father died during the night. His death was sudden and unexpected so my mother, now aged 78, is very distressed and I am unable to leave her at the moment.

I have arranged the funeral for Friday, so I shall be back at work on Monday.

I apologize for any inconvenience caused by my absence.

Yours sincerely
Graham Gorringe

Requesting a salary review

Dear Mr Frost

As you know, over the past 12 months I have taken on additional responsibilities within the department but this has not been reflected in my salary.

I would be grateful if you would consider reviewing my salary to take account of the extra work now involved in my job.

Yours sincerely
Sue Gubbins

Asking for promotion

Dear Mr Millichip

I understand that Mr Plant, the branch manager, is taking early retirement due to ill health and leaving at the end of April. I should like to apply for the position.

The two years I have spent as assistant manager have given me a thorough insight into the operation of a busy garden centre and I have a good working relationship with the junior members of staff.

As you know, I spent three months as acting manager last year while Mr Plant was in hospital and the centre ran smoothly and profitably within this time.

I should welcome the opportunity to discuss this with you.

Yours sincerely
Vanessa Bush

Expressing appreciation on retirement

Dear Sid

On the occasion of your retirement I felt that I must write to express my appreciation for the years of first-rate service you have given to the company. Your capable management and firm authority have meant that your department has always run smoothly and coped efficiently with an ever-increasing workload.

Though I am sure you have many plans for your retirement, I hope that you will be available for occasional assignments on a freelance basis. I will be in touch with you soon on this subject.

Meanwhile, I hope that retirement brings you all the pleasure and happiness you deserve.

Yours sincerely
Percy Grinder

Informal warning over unsatisfactory performance

Dear Tim

I have noticed, over the past few months, a marked deterioration in the standard of your work. Your last presentation was dull and pedestrian and showed all the hallmarks of a hastily prepared and slipshod piece of work.

You seem to have formed the habit of arriving late and leaving early. Three times over the past fortnight I have tried to contact you with queries between 4.30 and 5.30 pm, only to find that you had already left.

This is all the more disappointing because I have, in the past, found you one of our more self-disciplined and enthusiastic young executives.

Please let me know if there is some particular problem, within the office or outside, that is interfering with your whole-hearted commitment to your work. If so, perhaps we could talk over ways of improving the situation.

Yours sincerely
Bernard Boss

Excusing poor performance

Dear Bernard

I cannot argue with the contents of your letter. I am well aware that my performance over the past couple of months has been below standard.

Though I hesitate to offer excuses, I should explain that I have been going through a very difficult time recently, as my wife has been in and out of hospital for tests for a suspected neurological condition. She has been in a very distressed state and was keen that no-one should know of the problem until we had a definite diagnosis.

I am glad to say that the problem now seems to be sorted out and a successful treatment programme is under way.

Please accept my apologies for the apparent lack of commitment to my work during this time. From now onwards, I hope to be able to show you that your previous faith in my abilities was not misplaced.

Yours sincerely
Tim Earnest

Warning of possible dismissal for poor work

Dear Crispin

I am afraid that I must write this letter as a formal warning that over the past six months your work has fallen below the standards required by the company in several respects:

1. Your behaviour towards the staff in your department is authoritarian, producing resentment and a low standard of performance.
2. You have shown a nine-to-five outlook out of keeping with your position as sales manager.
3. You have shown impatience and tactlessness when dealing with customers, resulting in the cancellation of several orders.

I hope that following our discussions you will be able to live up to the standards expected of a sales manager in the future. I shall look for a substantial improvement in the coming month and will review the situation at the end of that time.

If this improvement is not forthcoming we shall be forced to dispense with your services.

Yours sincerely
Clarence Cross
Managing Director

Confirmation of dismissal

Dear Crispin

This is to confirm that you will be leaving the company on 31 June.

Your dismissal follows two warning letters dated 18 March and 20 April, drawing attention to your failure to discharge the responsibilities of your present post. Some of the specific instances of this poor performance have been discussed with you at length and are recorded in your personnel file.

I am sorry that this action has been necessary and wish you well in the future.

Yours sincerely
Clarence Cross

Formal notice of redundancy

Dear Arthur

I am sorry to have to tell you that, as part of the major reorganization of the company, due to take effect in April, it has been decided to close the machine tools section.

Unfortunately, it is not possible to find alternative work for the employees from this section within the works so I am forced to terminate your employment with Bulge and Blight with one month's notice on the grounds of redundancy. I enclose details of your redundancy and severance pay.

Rising costs and falling export sales have forced the company to take this difficult decision and the directors deeply regret having to part with loyal and hardworking staff in this manner.

May I take this opportunity of thanking you for the good service you have given the company over the past four years. I shall be happy to provide you with an excellent reference for any prospective employer. If I can assist you in any way in the future, please do not hesitate to get in touch.

Yours sincerely
Bartholomew Blight
Managing Director

Asking for voluntary redundancies

Dear Eddie

As you know, the company has faced several major setbacks this year. The recession in the industry as a whole has meant that too many firms are chasing too few orders. In the case of Tripp and Fall this means that we have to find ways of cutting costs in order to hold our own in a highly competitive market.

In short, we need to make 10 per cent staff cuts across the board. We hope that these reductions can be achieved by voluntary redundancy, so that no-one need feel disadvantaged. Details of the compensation offered to those willing to accept redundancy are attached and, as you will see, these terms are generous and well above the statutory minimum.

Those interested are invited to come and talk over the details in strictest confidence.

Yours sincerely
Theodore Tripp
Managing Director

Praising a member of staff for good work

Dear Rod

I feel I must write to express my appreciation for your excellent sales presentation last Friday.

A first presentation on this scale is always an ordeal but you handled it like a real pro. The clients were impressed by your imaginative flair, backed by sound research and I understand that a substantial order is in the pipeline.

Well done and keep up the good work!

Yours sincerely
Preston

Praising a departmental manager for organizational skill

Dear Rosamund

I must thank you for the skilful way in which you have handled the recent reorganization. I know that there have been times when you have had to exercize all your powers of tact and persuasion and the smooth transition to new methods of working was due largely to your efforts.

Please convey my thanks to every member of your department for the calm and professional way they have coped with the far-reaching changes.

Yours sincerely
Rupert

Thanking an employee for arranging a social occasion

Dear Melvyn

The annual dinner and dance was once again a resounding success. I have received many compliments from guests from outside the firm on the slick organization, the excellent catering and the enjoyable entertainment.

I know that none of this would have been possible without your hard work and your meticulous eye for detail.

Please accept my personal thanks for a job well done.

Yours sincerely
Gervase Bagshaw

7

Business Correspondence

A well-presented, precise letter is a good advertisement for the efficiency of your business. Plenty of business letters are still decked out in convoluted phrases like 'we respectfully beg to acknowledge receipt of your letter', 'owing to unforeseen circumstances' or 'assuring you of our best attention' but as a general rule, this kind of jargon is best avoided. If a single, well-chosen word will do the work of the whole phrase, then use it; it will express your meaning more accurately and it is less likely to sound as though you roll out the same old letter no matter what you have to say. The tone should always be courteous, even if you are disgusted with the person you are addressing. Never use sarcasm and, above all, never descend to abuse.

Always remember that you are writing to busy people with in-trays piled high. They will not thank you for wasting their time, so keep letters as short as possible, pruning out all inessentials. If someone else types your letter for you, check extra carefully to make sure that the words used are the words you intended, that the typing is accurate and that any enclosures are actually enclosed. Business letters must always be dated and if you have received a letter with a reference at the top, then it looks more efficient if you quote that reference in your correspondence.

Finance

Pressing for settlement of account (first reminder)

Dear Mr Bumstead

Account number ...

I write to call your attention to your account for £..., which is still outstanding from 3 September 19—.

We would be glad if you would settle the account as soon as possible.

Yours sincerely
Thomas Tight
Accounts Manager

Pressing for settlement of account (second reminder)

Dear Mr Bumstead

Account number ...

On 18 October I sent a reminder about your outstanding account for £... dated 3 September. As I have received no reply I must ask you to give this your urgent attention and forward a cheque at once.

Yours sincerely
Thomas Tight
Accounts Manager

Pressing for settlement of account (final reminder)

Dear Mr Bumstead

Account number ...

As I have sent two reminders about your outstanding account for £... dated 3 September, I write to inform you that unless I receive a cheque in full settlement within seven days of the date of this letter, the matter will be passed to our firm's solicitors for action.

Yours sincerely
Thomas Tight
Accounts Manager

Sending a cheque in settlement

Dear Mr Tight

I enclose my cheque for £... in settlement of account number ..., dated 3 September.

I do apologize for the delay which was due to an oversight.

Yours sincerely
Benedict Bumstead

Sending a cheque in part settlement of account

Dear Mr Tight

Account number ...

Thank you for your letter dated 10 November and reminder that our account dated 3 September is still outstanding.

I apologize for the delay, caused by a temporary cash flow problem. I enclose a cheque for £... in part payment. The remainder of the debt will be settled within the next seven days.

I trust that this delay will not cause you too much inconvenience. I shall take steps to ensure that future accounts are paid on time.

Yours sincerely
Benedict Bumstead

Asking for extra time to settle an account

Dear Mr Tight

Account number ...

I apologize for the delay in settling your account. The drop in the market has meant that several of our customers have been forced into liquidation, leaving several unpaid bills and resulting in a cash flow problem which I hope and believe will be only temporary.

Therefore I would ask you to allow us to postpone payment for a period of two months. By then our difficulties should be behind us and all outstanding accounts will be paid in full.

Yours sincerely
Benedict Bumstead

Querying an account

Dear Miss Merry

Account number ...

We return your invoice for 30 kitchen stools charged at £15.50 each. This seems to be a mistake.

Your quotation for the stools was £14.50 each. We would be grateful if you would confirm this and alter the invoice as necessary.

Prompt attention would be appreciated as we would be unable to accept the stools at the higher price.

Yours sincerely
Colin Chipchase
Purchasing Manager

Customers and orders

Enquiring about trade terms

Dear Sirs

I wish to order 5 dozen Executive Jet bath towels and 5 dozen Executive Jet hand towels. Please let me know your best trade terms for prompt settlement.

Yours faithfully
Betty Buyer (Miss)
Lots o' Linen

Notifying customer of trade terms

Dear Miss Buyer

Our price for trade supplies are as follows:

Executive Jet bath towels £.. per dozen
Executive Jet hand towels £... per dozen

We offer a discount of 5 per cent for cash settlement within 14 days of date of invoice and 2 per cent for settlement within 28 days.

We look forward to receiving your order and assure you of prompt attention.

Yours sincerely
Bradley Bulge
Sales Manager

Notifying a customer that a discount is not allowable

Dear Miss Buyer

Order ref....

Thank you for your cheque for £...

I see that you have subtracted 5 per cent discount but I must point out that this discount is only allowable on accounts settled within 14 days of the date of invoice. As your cheque was received 25 days after the date of invoice, the discount allowable is 2 per cent.

I should be grateful if you would send a cheque for the balance of £...

Yours sincerely
Bradley Bulge
Sales Manager

Sending a trade order

Dear Sirs

Order ref ...

Please supply the following office storage units:

2 work units PWBO 26D with doors
2 counter units PWBO 3DL without doors
4 shelved units DO 567

Please deliver to our warehouse at Docklands Road, Portsend.

Yours faithfully
Ferdinand Fixit
Supplies Manager

Acknowledging a trade order

Dear Mr Fixit

Order ref ...

In reply to your letter of 16 October, we are pleased to advise you that your order will be delivered to your warehouse on 4 November 19—.

Yours sincerely
Cassandra Clerk
Order Processing Department

Asking a customer to settle an account before supplying an order

Dear Mr Fixit

<u>Order ref ...</u>

Thank you for your order dated 16 October. We regret that we are unable to process your order until you have settled the overdue balance of £440 on your account.

As soon as your cheque arrives, we shall be pleased to supply further goods.

Yours sincerely
Theodore Tripp
Managing Director

Notifying customer of unavailability of goods ordered

Dear Mr Damp

Thank you for your order for 2 dozen Executive Jet bath towels, colour burgundy.

I am sorry to say that this line was discontinued six months ago. I enclose our current catalogues and colour samples. You will see that the nearest colour currently available is mulberry.

Please let me know whether or not you wish to order towels in an alternative colour.

Yours sincerely
Drusilla Dry
Order Processing Department

Enc.

Notifying a private customer of a price increase

Dear Mrs Spender

Thank you for your order of a Daredevil Bovverbike child's bicycle and your cheque for £85.

However, I am afraid that you have been looking at an out-of-date catalogue as the price for this bicycle is now £115.

Please let me know if you still wish to order this bicycle and if so, please forward the balance of £30. If you prefer to cancel your order, we will return your cheque.

Yours sincerely
Ronald Racer
Order Processing Department

Notifying trade customers of a price increase

Dear Sirs

Please note that there will be an across-the-board price increase of 5 per cent on all Scoffer Dog Food products with effect from 1 January 19—. Orders received before that date for supply during January will be supplied at pre-January 19— rates.

Yours faithfully
Wilfred Woof
Sales Manager

Taking up a trade reference

Dear Mr Winkles

Chipper and Fish Restaurants have given the name of your firm as a trade reference.

They have placed a first order with us and we would be obliged if you would let us know, in strict confidence, whether or not this company has proved reliable and prompt in settling past accounts with you.

We should be grateful for your assistance in this matter.

Yours sincerely
Winifred Plaice (Mrs)
General Manager

Supplying a trade reference

Dear Mrs Plaice

Thank you for your letter dated 11 January requesting a trade reference for Chipper and Fish Restaurants.

This firm has been a customer of ours for the past four years and has always settled accounts promptly. However, I would point out that their account with us has never stood at more than £500 at one time.

Yours sincerely
Wendell Winkles
Director

Refusing a trade reference

Dear Mrs Plaice

Thank you for your letter dated 2 July. I am sorry to say that I am unable to provide a trade reference for Chipper and Fish Restaurants at this time.

If you wish to discuss the matter further, please telephone me.

Yours sincerely
Wendell Winkles
Director

Requesting pre-payment

Dear Mr Suspect

Order ref. ...

Thank you for your order dated 10 April for 100 table lamps. This order is ready for delivery.

We regret that we cannot supply the goods on credit terms so we enclose our invoice and will dispatch the order immediately on receipt of your cheque.

Yours sincerely
Thomas Tight
Accounts Manager

Enquiring about an overdue order

Dear Mrs Tardy

Order ref. ...

I note that the delivery of this order is now one week overdue. Please contact me immediately to let me know the reasons for the delay and the date on which we may expect delivery.

Yours sincerely
Humphrey Quick
Purchasing Manager

Second enquiry about an overdue order

Dear Mrs Tardy

Order ref. ...

This order is now three weeks behind schedule and in spite of my letter dated 30 December we have received no explanation of the delay.

We now require delivery by 20 January or we have no choice but to cancel the order.

Yours sincerely
Humphrey Quick
Purchasing Manager

Apology for late delivery of order

Dear Mr Chaser

Order ref. ...

I regret to tell you that the above order for kitchen equipment will not be ready for dispatch on 22 October. This is due to circumstances beyond our control as our suppliers have been unable to meet agreed dates because of industrial action.

This action is now at an end and our revised delivery date is 18 November. I trust that this will not cause you too much inconvenience.

Yours sincerely
Myra Murch
Sales Director

Customer complaints

Replying to customer complaint of poor service

Dear Mrs Flurry

I was very sorry to hear of the discourteous treatment you received in Toogood Stores on 13 March.

In training our staff we stress the importance of good customer relations and we normally pride ourselves on a high standard of service. However, we certainly seem to have fallen down on this occasion. I have talked to the assistant involved and also to the department manager and I am confident that this unfortunate lapse will not be repeated.

In the meantime, please accept my sincere apologies for any annoyance and embarrassment that you have suffered.

Yours sincerely
Fiona Fulsome
Manager

Replying to customer complaint about unsatisfactory goods

Dear Mr Blotter

I am sorry to hear of the problems you have encountered with your Costapacket Copier. I have arranged for a service engineer to call on Monday morning and give the machine a thorough inspection and testing. He has been given strict instructions not to leave your premises without making certain that the machine is in full working order.

This copier is normally extremely reliable and I am sure that, once these teething troubles have been sorted out, you will be more than satisfied with its performance.

Do not hesitate to let me know if I can help in the future.

Yours sincerely
Barnabas Breeze
Customer Services

Rejecting a customer complaint about unsatisfactory goods

Dear Mr Gripe

Thank you for your letter dated 22 October, saying that the colour of the Dreamalot blankets did not match the colour sample sent to you with the catalogue.

I have examined the blanket you returned along with the sample and I have to advise you that any difference in colour is no more than can normally be expected between different batches of goods. I am afraid that, in the case of deep colours in particular, these slight shade variations do occur.

However, if you are not satisfied with the blankets, please return them and we will cancel your order. We hope to receive further orders from you in the future.

Yours sincerely
Brian Bedder
Sales Manager

Rejecting a persistent complaint

Dear Mr Winge

Thank you for your letter of 8 May.

I have investigated all the points you have raised in your previous letters and I must say that I can find no real justification for your complaints about the service given by my company.

We have been at pains to meet all your requests and regret that you are not satisfied by all our efforts.

I am sorry that I am unable to take matters further.

Yours sincerely
Thelma Tough
Director

Miscellaneous

Notifying clients of change of manager

Dear Miss Dabble

We write to tell you that our Marketing Director, Mr Sefton Seller, will be retiring on 30 April, after 15 years with the company. His successor is Mr Charles Creeper who comes to us from Buckle and Belt.

I am sure that he will be in touch with you in the near future and will wish to maintain the close and longstanding relationship between our two firms.

With kind regards
Yours sincerely
Marcus Major

Notifying clients of a death

Dear Charles

It is with great regret that I have to tell you of the sudden death of one of our account executives, Graham Brown. He was a tremendous asset to the firm and we shall sadly miss him.

For the time being, I shall be handling Graham's accounts so please contact me with any matters needing attention.

Yours sincerely
Sydney Stiff

Notifying customers of change of address

Dear Customer

Change of address

We are pleased to announce that we are moving to larger premises. From 1 April our address will be:

SNAP-IT PHOTOGRAPHY
21 CAMERA STREET
SHUTTERDOWN
PORTSEND
PL5 2DF

Our new store will enable us to offer an extended range of top quality goods as well as the fast and efficient service you have come to expect.

Yours faithfully
Ranulf Snapper

Circular notifying change of ownership

Dear Customer

We are pleased to tell you that Sudsit Laundries, 54 High Street, Downtown, will in future be operating as a branch of Dazzle White, Dazzle Bright Dry Cleaners and Launderers. We pride ourselves on our high standard laundry and dry cleaning service for personal and business customers, hotels and restaurants.

In addition we offer:

* 2 hour dry cleaning service
* fast and skilful repair service
* specialist suede and leather cleaning

We hope to have the pleasure of serving you in the near future.

Yours faithfully
Beatrice Bright

Notifying potential customers of a new business

Dear Householder

We would like to tell you of a new service in your area.

Tart-It-Up Decorators have been trading successfully in Downtown and Churchdown for the past five years and are now able to offer the same high quality of work in Portsend.

We can provide, at reasonable prices:

* Interior and exterior paintwork
* Paperhanging
* French polishing

There are no cowboys here. Every one of our staff is City and Guilds qualified. Estimates are free and our service is friendly and reliable.

Phone now for a personal estimate that will delight you.

Yours faithfully
Sandy Sharp

8

Invitations and Replies

Invitations should be as formal or informal as the coming event. There are traditional forms of wording for formal invitations and these are usually printed but if the number of guests is small, or you prefer a more personal form of words, invitations can be handwritten or in the form of a personal note. However you choose to issue the invitation, it should always give the place, the time and the date – though it is not necessary to give the year – and the address to which a reply should be sent.

Weddings

Invitation to a formal wedding

Mr and Mrs Benjamin Budd
request the pleasure of the company of

————

at the marriage of their daughter
Rose
with
Mr Charles Bachelor
at
St Saviour's Church, Downtown
on Saturday, 11th July
at 3 o'clock
and afterwards at the George Hotel, Downtown

R.S.V.P.
address

OR

Mr John Smith (name of person invited)

Mr and Mrs Benjamin Budd
request the pleasure of
your company at the marriage of their daughter
Rose
to
Mr Charles Bachelor
at St Saviour's Church, Downtown
on Saturday, 11th July
at 3 o'clock
and afterwards at the
George Hotel, Downtown

R.S.V.P.
address

Invitation to a formal wedding where the bride is hostess

Miss Anne Smith (name of person invited)

Miss Rose Budd
requests the pleasure of your company
at her marriage to
Mr Charles Bachelor
St Saviour's Church, etc.

Invitation to a formal wedding if the bride and groom are joint hosts

Mrs Letty Smith

Mr Charles Bachelor and Miss Rose Budd
request the pleasure of your company at their marriage, etc.

Invitation to a formal wedding when relative, rather than the girl's parents, is acting as host

Mr Tom Smith

Mr and Mrs Basil Bacon
request the pleasure of your company
at the marriage of their niece
Rose Budd, etc.

117

Invitation to a formal wedding if the groom's parents are arranging and paying for the wedding

Mr and Mrs Dominic Bachelor
request the pleasure of the company of

_____

at the marriage of
Miss Rose Budd
to
their son Charles, etc.

Invitation to a formal wedding where the bride's parents are divorced

Mr Benjamin Budd and Mrs Jenny Budd
request the pleasure, etc.

Or, if the wife has remarried

Mr Benjamin Budd and Mrs Brian Birtwhistle
request the pleasure, etc.

Invitation to a double wedding

Miss Jane Smith

Mr and Mrs Winter-Evans
request the pleasure of your company
at the marriage of their daughters
Alison
with
Mr James Carrington
and
Emma
with
Mr Geoffrey Champion
at St Michael's Church, etc.

Formal invitation to the wedding reception only

Mr and Mrs Albert Smith

Mr and Mrs Benjamin Budd
request the pleasure of your company
at a reception to follow the marriage of their daughter
Rose
with
Mr Charles Bachelor
at the George Hotel, Downtown
on Saturday 11th July at 1.30 pm

Informal invitation to a wedding and reception where the bride and groom are hosts

Charles and Rose invite .... to their marriage at St Saviour's Church on Saturday 11 July at 3 o'clock and to a party afterwards at Flat 5, The Willows, Abingdon Road etc.

Accepting a formal invitation

Miss Barbara Bliss has much pleasure in accepting the kind invitation of Mr and Mrs Budd to the marriage of their daughter on Saturday, 11 July at St Saviour's Church and afterwards at The George Hotel, Downtown.

Refusing a formal invitation

Miss Barbara Bliss thanks Mr and Mrs Budd for their kind invitation to the marriage of their daughter Rose but regrets that a prior engage-ment prevents her from accepting.

Accepting an informal invitation

Nigel and Diedre will be delighted to accept the invitation to your wedding on Saturday 11 July.

Parties

Invitation to a formal dinner party

Colonel and Mrs Blenkinsop

request the pleasure of your company

at dinner

on Saturday 6th June

at 8.30 pm

RSVP
address

Invitation to a semi-formal dinner party

Dear Mrs Peach

We are having a small dinner party on Saturday, 6 June at 8 pm and
hope that you and Mr Peach will give us the pleasure of your
company.

Yours sincerely
Amanda Blenkinsop

Invitation to a formal cocktail party

Mr and Mrs Percy Philpott

Mrs Isabel Glendenning

at Home

Saturday 6th June

RSVP   Cocktails
address   6.30 pm

Formal invitation to son's 18th birthday celebrations

Dr and Mrs Peter Glendenning

request the pleasure of the company of

_____

on the occasion of the 18th birthday

of their son Mark

at the Pink Elephant, Townford

on Saturday 8th August

at 8pm

RSVP
address

Disco
8.30 pm

Formal invitation to daughter's engagement party

Miss Peggy Philpott

Mr and Mrs Andrew Branch

request the pleasure of your company

at a party

to celebrate the engagement

of their daughter Bridget

to Tony Twigg

on Saturday 6th June

at The Barley Mow Hotel

RSVP
address

Dancing
8 pm

OR

Tony Twigg and Bridget Branch

request the pleasure of the company of

_____

at a party to celebrate their engagement, etc.

Formal invitation to a company function

The Directors of Pushit Advertising

request the pleasure of the company of

————————

at their annual dinner and dance

at the Grand Hotel, Townford

on Saturday 6th June

at 8 pm

RSVP

Abigail Arnley-Smith
Pushit Advertising   Black tie
address

Semi-formal invitation to a company function

Dear Rosemary,

The firm is holding its annual dinner and dance on Saturday 6 June and I would be delighted if you would be my guest for the evening. It's an evening dress affair at the Grand Hotel and if you would like to come, I will call for you at about 7.45 pm.

Yours,
Tony

Accepting a formal party invitation

Mr and Mrs Woodrow Willis thank Colonel and Mrs Blenkinsop for their kind invitation to dinner, *etc.*, on Saturday, 6 June and will be happy to accept.

Accepting a semi-formal party invitation

Dear Mrs Blenkinsop

Thank you very much for your invitation to dinner on 6 June. Mr Peach and I would be delighted to accept.

Yours sincerely
Pearl Peach

Refusing a formal party invitation

Miss Peggy Philpott thanks Colonel and Mrs Blenkinsop for their kind invitation to dinner on Saturday 6 June but regrets that a prior engagement prevents her from accepting (*or* regrets that she is unable to accept due to family commitments).

Refusing a semi-formal party invitation

Dear Mrs Blenkinsop

Thank you very much for your invitation to dinner on Saturday 6 June. I am afraid that John and I are unable to accept as we shall be away on holiday at the time.

It was very kind of you to think of us and I only wish that the dates had not clashed.

Yours sincerely
Pearl Peach

Miscellaneous

Invitation to relatives to spend Christmas

Dear Uncle Wilf and Auntie Flo,

Gavin and I would love you to come and spend Christmas with us this year. We don't see nearly enough of you and it would be a good opportunity to catch up on all the family news.

We would all go to Mum and Dad for Christmas lunch and on Boxing Day Gavin's parents will be coming for dinner. Apart from that, it will be just us and the kids and far too much to eat and drink!

If you can come – and we do hope you can – we suggest that you arrive for supper on Christmas Eve.

Love,
Mavis

Accepting an invitation for Christmas

Dear Mavis,

Thank you very much for inviting us to spend Christmas with you. We can't imagine a nicer way to celebrate and we shall look forward to seeing you.

Auntie would like to bring a Christmas cake as our contribution. You know how much she loves baking and she has a treasured recipe handed down from her mother's mother.

Traffic permitting, we should arrive about 7 pm on Christmas Eve.

> With love,
> Uncle Wilf and Auntie Flo

Refusing an invitation for Christmas

Dear Mavis,

It was very kind of you to ask us to spend Christmas with you. Sadly, we shall not be able to come this year. As you know, Auntie Flo's arthritis has been getting worse recently and she doesn't feel that she can face the journey in winter temperatures, so we think it would be wise to spend the holiday quietly at home. If only you were nearer!

We shall certainly be thinking of you and hope we can fix a get-together in the summer.

> With love,
> Uncle Wilf and Auntie Flo

Writing to ask a girl for a date

Dear Jemima,

I shall be home in Portsend over the weekend of 22-24 May and wonder if you would like to go to the theatre with me on the Saturday evening. The Repertory Theatre is putting on *Private Lives* and I'm sure it will be worth seeing.

It begins at 8pm so, if you are free, perhaps I could pick you up at 6.30 pm and we could have a bite to eat first.

> All the best,
> Nigel

Accepting a date

Dear Nigel,

What a lovely idea! I'm really pleased that you thought of me and I shall look forward to seeing you.

I've promised to help a friend with a children's party in the afternoon, so 6.30 pm might be cutting it a bit fine. Could you make it 7.30 pm instead and then come back here for a snack supper after the show? Let me know if the idea appeals.

> All the best,
> Jemima

Refusing a date

Dear Nigel,

It was very nice of you to think of me but I'm afraid I won't be able to accept your invitation to the theatre, as I have already promised to spend that weekend with friends.

I hope you enjoy your visit home.

> All the best,
> Jemima

Forms of Address

The Queen
Envelope: Her Majesty the Queen
Beginning: Madam
Ending: I have the honour to be, Madam,
Your Majesty's most humble and obedient servant

Princes and Princesses
Envelope: His Royal Highness, the Prince Andrew *or* Her Royal Highness, the Princess Michael of Kent
Beginning: Sir or Madam
Ending: I have the honour to be, Sir (Madam), Your Royal Highness's most humble and obedient servant

Dukes and Duchesses
Envelope: His Grace the Duke of Birmingham *or* Her Grace the Duchess of Birmingham
Beginning: My Lord Duke *or* Dear Madam
Ending: Yours faithfully

Other Peers
Envelope: The Most Hon. the Marquess of Portsend
The Rt Hon. the Earl of Downtown
The Rt Hon. the Viscount Poppleford
The Rt Hon. the Lord Burpford
Beginning: My Lord
Ending: Yours faithfully

Wives of peers
Envelope: The Most Hon. the Marchioness of Portsend
The Rt Hon. the Countess of Downtown
The Rt Hon. the Viscountess Poppleford
The Rt Hon. the Lady Burpford
Beginning: Dear Madam
Ending: Yours faithfully

Baronet
Envelope: Sir Murgatroyd Mortiboys, Bt
Beginning: Dear Sir
Ending: Yours faithfully

Baronet's Wife
Envelope: Lady Mortiboys
Beginning: Dear Madam
Ending: Yours faithfully

Knight
Envelope: Sir Farley Funtington, GCB (*or* other)
Beginning: Dear Sir
Ending: Yours faithfully

Knight's wife
Envelope: Lady Funtington
Beginning: Dear Madam
Ending: Yours faithfully

Dame
Envelope: Dame Claribel Carruthers, DCB (*or* other)
Beginning: Dear Madam
Ending: Yours faithfully

The Prime Minister
Envelope: The Right Hon. Benedict Birtwhistle, MP
Beginning: Dear Sir or Dear Madam. (Dear Prime Minister should only be used if you know the Prime Minister socially)
Ending: Yours faithfully

Government Ministers	*Envelope:* The Rt Hon. Cuthbert Clutterbuck, MP, Secretary of State for Education *or* Secretary of State for Education *Beginning:* Dear Mr Clutterbuck *or* Mrs Clutterbuck *or* Miss Clutterbuck *Ending:* Yours sincerely
Members of Parliament	*Envelope:* The Rt Hon. Cuthbert Clutterbuck, MP *Beginning:* Dear Mr Clutterbuck (*or* Mrs Clutterbuck *or* Miss Clutterbuck) *Ending:* Yours sincerely
The Lord Chancellor	*Envelope:* The Rt Hon. The Lord Chancellor *Beginning:* My Lord *Ending:* Yours faithfully
The Lord Chief Justice	*Envelope:* The Rt Hon. the Lord Chief Justice of England *Beginning:* My Lord *Ending:* Yours faithfully
Lord Justice of the Court of Appeal	*Envelope:* The Rt Hon. Lord Justice Dumbleton *Beginning:* My Lord *Ending:* Yours faithfully
High Court Judge	*Envelope:* The Hon. Mr Justice Dumbleton *or* The Hon. Mrs Justice Dumbleton (this is used for both married and unmarried women) *Beginning:* Dear Sir *or* Dear Madam *Ending:* Yours faithfully
Circuit Judge	*Envelope:* His Honour Judge Bloomer *or* Her Honour Judge Bloomer *Beginning:* Dear Sir *or* Dear Madam *Ending:* Yours faithfully
Archbishop	*Envelope:* The Most Reverend the Lord Archbishop of Canterbury *Beginning:* My Lord Archbishop *Ending:* Yours faithfully
Bishop	*Envelope:* The Right Reverend the Lord Bishop of Bartleford *Beginning:* My Lord Bishop *Ending:* Yours faithfully
Dean	*Envelope:* The Very Reverend the Dean of Bartleford *Beginning:* Very Reverend Sir *Ending:* Yours faithfully
Archdeacon	*Envelope:* The Venerable the Archdeacon of Bartleford *Beginning:* Venerable Sir *Ending:* Yours faithfully
Canon	*Envelope:* The Reverend Canon Arthur Dibbs *Beginning:* Dear Canon *or* Dear Canon Dibbs *Ending:* Yours faithfully *or* Yours sincerely

Vicar	*Envelope:* The Reverend Clarence Good *Beginning:* Dear Vicar *or* Dear Mr Good *Ending:* Yours sincerely
Roman Catholic Priest	*Envelope:* The Reverend Patrick Murphy *Beginning:* Dear Father Murphy *Ending:* Yours sincerely
Jewish Rabbi	*Envelope:* Rabbi David Goldberg *Beginning:* Dear Rabbi Goldberg *Ending:* Yours sincerely
Armed Forces Officers	*Envelope:* Rank is used as appropriate, with decorations or distinctions: Captain William Woburn, CBE, RN Lieutenant Sebastian Hamilton, RN Field Marshall Sir Dugald Dainty, KCB, CBE Major Harold Hackett, MC Air Commodore Cedric Chipperfield, DFC, RAF Flying Officer Rupert Winger, RAF (For the Royal Navy, below the rank of Rear-Admiral, add RN after decorations. For the Royal Air Force, ranks below Air Commodore have RAF after name and decorations.) *Beginning:* Dear Sir *or* Dear Major Hackett *Ending:* Yours faithfully *or* Yours sincerely
Chairman of County (or District) Council	*Envelope:* The Chairman of Ripford County (*or* District) Council *Beginning:* Dear Mr Chairman (for men or women) *Ending:* Yours faithfully
Lord Mayor	*Envelope:* The Right Honourable the Lord Mayor of Portsend *Beginning:* My Lord Mayor (for men or women) *Ending:* Yours faithfully
Lady Mayoress	*Envelope:* The Lady Mayoress of Portsend *Beginning:* My Lady Mayoress *Ending:* Yours faithfully
Mayor	*Envelope:* The Right Worshipful the Mayor of Downtown *Beginning:* Mr Mayor *Ending:* Yours faithfully
Mayoress	*Envelope:* The Mayoress of Downtown *Beginning:* Madam Mayoress *Ending:* Yours faithfully
Doctor of Medicine	*Envelope:* Dr Bradley Sprunt or B. Sprunt, Esq., MD *Beginning:* Dear Dr Sprunt *Ending:* Yours sincerely
Head Teacher	*Envelope:* Mr Ernest Wiseman, Headmaster (*or* Principal) *or* Mrs (Miss) Bertha Wiseman, Headmistress (*or* Principal) *Beginning:* Dear Mr (Mrs *or* Miss) Wiseman *Ending:* Yours sincerely